Volunteers Working with Young Readers

Volunteers
Working with Young Readers

Lester L. Laminack   *Western Carolina University*

National Council of Teachers of English   ◆   1111 W. Kenyon Road, Urbana, Illinois 61801-1096

Staff Editor: Zarina M. Hock
Interior and Cover Design: Jenny Jensen Greenleaf

For permissions, see page x.

NCTE Stock Number: 34106-3050

Library of Congress Cataloging-in-Publication Data
Laminack, Lester L., 1956–
    Volunteers working with young readers / Lester L. Laminack.
      p. cm.
    Includes bibliographical references (p.).
    ISBN 0-8141-3410-6
    1. Volunteer workers in education—United States.   2. Reading teachers—United States.   3. Reading (Elementary)—United States—Language experience approach.   I. Title.
    LB2844.1.V6L36   1998
    371.41—dc21   98-15541
                                              CIP

For Ruth Johnson Colvin,
founder of Literacy Volunteers of America, Inc.,
a woman who has dedicated her life to helping volunteers serve adults
who have the courage to ask for help. In all her work, the learner has
always come first. I have met no one with her energy, few
with her commitment, and fewer still with her
passion for helping those in need.

And

For Mrs. Hand, my elementary school librarian, whose voice
was the magic carpet on which I rode into many a story.

And also

For all the young children who need a bit of extra support
and those adults who are willing to give it.

Contents

Acknowledgments

There are many significant folks who helped along the way as *Volunteers Working with Young Readers* came to be.

First, I must thank my family, Glenda and Zachary, who let me retreat to my study when I needed the time to write. I also owe a great debt to the many children and teachers from whom I have learned during my career. I am constantly amazed by the smart things that children do in the process of learning to read and write. I am equally amazed by the wise ways that teachers support that development with such grace and caring.

Next, I want to thank Karen Smith and Michael Greer for sharing my excitement for this project from the point of the first discussion. And for introducing me to Pete Feely, who guided me through the entire process, served as a springboard for ideas, and was always supportive and encouraging when I was pressed for time (congratulations to Pete who became a father for the second time during the production of the book).

Zarina Hock, thank you for your able and cheerful assistance in pulling the threads together into a lovely fabric. This book would not have been the same without your watchful eye.

Permissions

Introduction

Reading is one of those things most of us take for granted. For many of us it is effortless, unconscious, natural—something we do with very little thought or struggle. We see print and move fluidly to ideas on the rhythms and cadences of language.

Most children come to reading rather easily, some with more struggle than others. In classrooms where young children are growing into readers and writers there are many interactions with print. Well-informed teachers are constantly demonstrating how print works in our world and leading children to discover the connections between their knowledge of language as used in life and the world represented in print.

As a volunteer you will be participating in that exciting phase in the lives of young children when they develop individual identities as readers and writers. Clearly, that identity is crucial to the child's growth. Seeing themselves as "doers," as readers and writers, provides a stepping stone for children as they learn to make use of their knowledge of how oral language works in the process of switching "codes" to written language.

Most of us think the act of reading is something anyone can teach—after all, we know how to do it. What could be so hard? Take a few minutes here to think through your responses to these questions and jot down your ideas:

1. What is reading?
2. When is a child ready to learn to read?
3. What are the essential materials needed for teaching a child to read?
4. What methods, techniques, and strategies do you think are the most important for beginning?

Your Own Reading History

Do you remember learning to read at school? Chances are that your views of reading and how it should be taught are influenced by your own experiences as a student. Perhaps you remember reading about Dick and Jane, or Alice and Jerry, or Buffy and Mack. If your class was like many others throughout the country, there were three reading groups organized into levels by ability. A high group, an average group, and a low group. You might even recall which group you were a member of. Maybe you even remember the group name, the Tigers, the Green Turtles, or the like.

Usually, each of the three groups met with the teacher for about thirty minutes while the others worked in their seats. This work often included completing pages in workbooks, board work, and assorted worksheets. Perhaps you can recall sitting in the circle counting the number of lines on the page to figure out when you would be called on to read aloud while your teacher and classmates followed along in their copies of the book.

If you share that memory with me, then you probably also recall the student who would interrupt your reading and point out a word you misread. At times, your teacher would, too. Each new "story" usually had three or four more words than the previous selection. And the teacher would begin the lesson with the new words you'd find in the selection. Then, when the selection was finished and everyone in the group had taken a turn reading aloud, the teacher would turn a page in her book and ask several questions.

Keep your experience in mind. How much rings true with your memory? Notice how much of this experience is focused on words. It is clear that many adults have similar experiences, and we must recognize the tremendous influence of our histories as students upon our beliefs about teaching, volunteering as tutors, and the role of schools. If our memories of learning to read are crowded by workbooks, worksheets, and activities focused on finding the missing vowel, filling in the initial sound, locating the word with the same pronunciation or meaning, then we too might think of those activities as important for students. If we recall sitting in circles organized by ability, then we might believe that good literacy instruction requires sorting children into levels. If we can remember reading aloud in those circles and having someone call our attention to a word we overlooked or mis-read, then we might believe that getting the words right is the single most important task for a reader. If our reading circle always ended with the teacher turning the page and asking questions about details in the story, then we might believe that comprehension means giving the right answers to someone else's questions.

Three Views of Reading

Now, consider this. Most definitions of reading or literacy will fall into one of three broad views of what it means to become a reader (Weaver, 1994):

- View one: Learning to read means learning to pronounce words
- View two: Learning to read means learning to identify words and get their meanings
- View three: Learning to read means bringing meaning to the text in order to construct or make meaning from the text.

Each of these views is based on some basic assumptions about what readers and writers do.

View one, learning to pronounce words, is based on the assumption that "breaking the code" or learning to "sound out" words is the most essential skill for students. It is assumed that comprehension will occur when the student is able to pronounce the word.

View two, learning to identify words and get their meanings, is based on the assumption that reading is again a word-level activity. The essential skill is word identification and vocabulary development. In other words, getting the word and getting its meaning is the basic task of a reader. The assumption here is that the meaning of the story, article, report, or text will become clear if the student can identify all the words and knows what each word means.

View three, learning to bring meaning to a text in order to construct or make meaning from the text, is based on the assumption that meaning does not lie in the print. Learning to utilize the prior knowledge, experiences, and understanding of language to make sense of the print is the essential skill here. The assumption is that reading is an active mental process that results in understanding. It is further assumed that this understanding does not necessarily come from the precise identification of every letter or word or even from knowing the definition of each word. Rather, reading is an interplay between the ideas, experiences, and language of a writer and a reader. It is through that interplay that readers broaden their understandings and construct meaning for themselves.

So, at this point you're probably thinking about where your definition fits, and you may be trying to choose sides. Whoa, not yet! This is

not an either-or situation. Maybe you don't need to choose. Let's look more closely.

Try thinking about the three views as a great pyramid standing in the desert. As we travel across the desert in search of wisdom, crossing tall dunes we see in the distance the peak of the great pyramid. From our vantage point, however, it appears to be a small pyramid resting on a large dune far ahead. View one, the tip of the pyramid, is something like that. It could be seen as a stand-alone perspective, complete, whole, self-sufficient; a pyramid unto itself. Clearly, those who hold this view believe that phonics—learning to pronounce words or sounding words out—is the single most important skill young students need to become independent readers. And indeed, phonics is an important tool in a reader's repertoire of strategies. However, this perspective of literacy is limited. Remember the pyramid we could see in the distance and how we were only seeing the peak? Remember how we could assume that the peak was a small pyramid standing alone on a dune in the distance just because we couldn't see the whole pyramid from where we stood? In many ways, thinking of reading as the act of pronouncing words is just as limited. When we take the stand that sounding out words is *the* essential skill required of a reader, we position ourselves in ways that prevent us from seeing the value of developing other word identification and recognition strategies, building vocabulary, and building on the student's knowledge, experience, and language.

Back to the desert and the search for wisdom in the great pyramid. As we cross other high dunes and draw nearer to the great pyramid, we begin to see that the pyramid is larger than we first thought. In fact, it seems to have a broader base and nearly doubles in size as it sits on a far off dune. View two, the middle layer of that pyramid, may indeed look like the base from our current vantage point. This middle layer broadens the whole, though it doesn't appear as a pyramid unto itself. Rather, it supports the tip, broadening the entire pyramid. It doesn't negate or replace the tip. It simply makes the tip, once viewed as a whole, part of something even greater. What's the connection to reading? View two, identifying words and getting their meaning subsumes view one, learning to pronounce words. Think about this: learning to pronounce words (phonics or sounding out words) is ONE way to identify words. From the perspective of view two, the issue is twofold. First, identifying the word, through whatever means. This could include phonics, syllabication (breaking words into syllables), using context, or any other strategy that would result in getting the word right. The issue is getting the correct pronunciation of the word. The second is getting the meaning of the word which usually implies attention to vocabulary development. Both these issues include and broaden the scope of view one. As we keep traveling through the desert crossing dune after dune, we find ourselves within sight of the great pyramid. From this vantage point we now see the entire pyramid resting on a great broad base. It is clear that the pyramid is nearly three times the size we first thought. View three, learning to bring meaning to the text in order to construct or make meaning from the text, is like that broad foundation, the massive base supporting the whole pyramid. In this role, view three takes in the contributions of views one and two. Clearly, the goal of a reader is to make sense of the ideas presented in the written language. Toward this goal a reader must have an array of skills and strategies for making sense of print, including word-identification skills and vocabulary development. In addition, the reader must rely on all of his or her prior experiences, language, and sense of self as a reader or writer. In order to make sense of what is written or to build a personally relevant understanding, the readers must have

- strategies for identifying unfamiliar words
- a growing vocabulary in the language they are trying to read
- experiences to draw upon and connect with when considering the ideas of others
- language use

It is clear then, that view three does not exclude nor negate the existence of views one and two. Rather, view three places them in a context, providing a frame for their existence in the whole.

CHAPTER 1

Volunteers in the Classroom

How Can You Help?
Your First Days as a Volunteer

So you're all ready to jump in there and help a child on the way to becoming a proficient reader. Thank you. Teachers appreciate willing volunteers in their busy days and crowded classrooms. If you are volunteering in a classroom, remember that the teacher is responsible for all the children in that class. Therefore, you should always work closely with the teacher in planning your visits and in devising an assessment plan that can guide your work with a child or group. The classroom teacher will have the greatest insight into the individual needs of each child and the specific requirements of the curriculum. You would be wise to use the teacher's knowledge as one of your primary resources.

In the classroom, there will be children who are very proficient readers for their age. Those children can often function independently. Other children will be making average- to slightly less-than-average

> ≺ IN THIS SECTION
>
> - *Reading aloud to the class, to a small group, or to an individual child*
> - *Listening to a child read aloud*
> - *Working with a small group over time*
> - *Working with an individual child over time*

progress in their development as readers and writers. While still others may be struggling with reading. It is my opinion that your role as a volunteer in the classroom should be to work with those children who are making slightly less-than-average progress. Those very proficient readers can either work independently or with peers making average or better progress. Your work with slightly below-average students frees the teacher to work with those students who are struggling most. In essence, your presence not only provides much-needed individual and small-group instruction for specific children, it also provides the most highly skilled professional in the classroom with an opportunity to maximize time spent with the least proficient, most "in-need" students in the class.

So maybe you're wondering what you'll be doing when you volunteer your time. There are several ways you can be helpful.

Some Possibilities

What follows is a list of possibilities for your involvement. This list is intended to provide some general guidance as you begin your work as a volunteer.

1. Reading aloud to the class, to a small group, or to an individual child (your reading partner)
- choose books you enjoy
- always rehearse the book aloud before reading for an audience

- remember to give the title as well as the name(s) of the author and illustrator
- use your voice to set the tone or mood of the story
- use your voice to bring the characters to life

2. Listening to a child read aloud
- invite the child to bring something to read for you each time
- listen without interrupting the reader
- expect the child to have a rationale for the selection
- support the child's strategies for making sense of print
- resist the urge to correct every misread word
- make a note when the child struggles with a word or misreads a word that alters meaning

3. Working with a small group over time
- participate in a literature circle
- assist in locating books and other material for literature circles, author studies, genre studies, or topic studies
- participate in an inquiry project
- assist in recording what is known about the topic
- assist in generating and recording questions for inquiry
- assist the group in making connections between the topic and materials they have previously read
- assist in writing a script for a play, producing the play, and performing the play

4. Working with an individual child over time

- read aloud to the child
- listen to the child read
- help the child locate other titles of interest
- assist in making connections between books
- demonstrate reading strategies that will broaden the child's repertoire

Now let's take each of these activities and open them up a bit. The following elaboration may give you a deeper understanding of each of the possibilities listed above.

Reading Aloud to the Class, to a Small Group, or to an Individual Child (Your Reading Partner)

When I was in elementary school I used to look forward to "library day," that day when my class got to go to the library for the selection of new books. But, selecting a new book was not the thing I looked forward to most about library day. I longed for the voice of Mrs. Hand, our librarian. She could take any story to new heights through her careful, thoughtful, and casually dramatic rendering of text. Her voice was smooth, velvety, and a little deep for a woman, I always thought. A voice something like that of actress Patricia Neal. She could make us tremble at the scary parts. Bring tears at the sad parts. Send us reeling at the humor. She could draw us up to the edge of our seats and nearly have us teetering on the brink of disaster at the dangerous feats of our heroes.

It was in that library sitting in the presence of Mrs. Hand, wrapped in the velvet cloak that was her voice that I believed myself into reading my first chapter book. Mrs. Hand would read just a chapter of *The Boxcar Children* and leave us suspended in space until the next Thursday. All week we talked about Henry, Jesse, Violet, and little Benny hiding out in that boxcar. All week we pretended to be them in the woods at the edge of our school yard. All week we guessed and plotted out what would happen next. Mrs. Hand taught me to hold a story in my hands, to carry it with me throughout the week. She taught me to relish the events of a fictitious place, to go there and visit with my new friends. I will never forget her voice, her love of books, her love for children nor her gift of reading aloud.

Reading aloud to children in groups or as individuals plays an important role in their overall literacy development. This seemingly simple and rather pleasurable act accomplishes so much with so little effort. Being read to allows children the opportunity to become familiar with the language of story, poetry, information books, pamphlets, directions, etc. In addition, it is through the experience of listening to an engaging reader that children first begin to grasp the notion that those marks on the page tell fascinating stories. The act of reading aloud to children demonstrates how written language should sound, what readers do with phrasing, intonation, inflection to bring life to otherwise still and quiet print. Through repeated readings of favorite stories, children come to understand that the print tells the story, that print is stable and says the same thing each time it is read. Rereading could also allow you to discover more meaning in the same words. Reading aloud allows children to see and hear how language can be organized in various forms to accomplish a variety of purposes for different audiences. For example, the language in a *Frog and Toad* story is organized differently than the language of a pamphlet for the hands-on science museum the class will visit next month on a field trip. The language of a predictable book such as *Brown Bear, Brown Bear* is organized differently than the language of a traditional tale such as *Goldilocks and the Three Bears*.

It is through repeated exposure to such language that children first begin to explore the possibility of using different forms in their own writing. In each meeting with your reading partner plan some time to read aloud for the child's pleasure. It's valuable instruction without pain. Here are some things to keep in mind when reading aloud to children. Read the story or text yourself a few times and rehearse it aloud before sharing it with an audience, even an audience of one. Know where you need to slow down, where a word needs to stretch, where you need to increase the speed or volume a bit. Know where your voice needs to rise and fall. Note the use of punctuation, line breaks, bold print and other conventions of print as signals to how the language should sound. All these things enhance the delivery of the story, engage the listener, and bring the characters to life. In *A Sense of Wonder* (1995) Katherine Paterson has said, "'Let me hear you read it' is a test. 'Let me read it to you' is a gift" (pp. 281–282). In short, think of your reading aloud as a gift. Select carefully with knowledge of the recipient in mind; package it beautifully and present it with love.

Jim Trelease (1982) in his now famous book, *The Read-Aloud Handbook*, offers some additional advice, which I have summarized below, combining it with my own suggestions on the subject.

- The art of listening is taught and cultivated gradually.
- Don't feel that you have to tie every book to classwork.
- Don't overwhelm the audience. When choosing a book you should consider the intellectual, social, and emotional level of your audience.
- Don't read stories that you don't enjoy yourself.
- Don't start unless you have time to do justice to the story.
- Adjust your pace to fit the story.
- Reluctant readers or unusually active children frequently find it difficult to just sit and listen. Paper, crayons, and pencils allow them to keep their hands busy while listening.
- Don't be fooled by awards. Not all award-winning books make good read-alouds.
- Use plenty of expression when reading. Change the tone of your voice to fit the dialogue or set the mood when possible.

Listening to a Child Read Aloud

A good listener is hard to find. Too often, children view the act of reading aloud to an adult as a test of some sort. Many children, especially those who are developing more slowly as readers, are asked to read to an adult only for the adult to assess progress. At each meeting with your young partner, invite the child to select something to read to you. Let the child know you expect to hear why he or she picked this selection to read for you. Therefore, at each meeting, before you begin to read aloud to the child, you should introduce your selection (book, story, poem, etc.) and also tell why you chose it. For example, "I found the most beautiful book to read for you today. It's called *All the Places to Love*. I just love the way this sounds, just listen. And the pictures are so real. It makes me feel as if I could step into the book. I chose this one because it reminds me of my visits to my grandmother's farm when I was little. I hope you enjoy it."

By doing this each time you read aloud for the child, you repeat a demonstration that will help your young partner learn the possibilities for how books are selected, the reasons for sharing, and the driving force behind our pleasures in reading aloud.

When the child presents his or her selection remember to be a good listener. Focus on the selection and the child's reasons for choosing it. The child may choose a piece because it is very funny. Then you validate the humor. Perhaps because of the rich description, in which case you validate the image-rich language. Maybe the selection was chosen because it was confusing. Then, you note the confusion and help to clarify. Whatever the rationale, try to help support the child's growing sense of self as reader and writer. Try to help the child grow into the literate life he or she has envisioned. Support strategies for making selections and continue to offer demonstrations of how you do that yourself.

As the child reads aloud to you, accept the gift graciously and don't turn the event into an evaluation. Resist the urge to correct every misread word. Encourage the child to ask her- or himself if the language is making sense. You might note on an index card or a sticky note when the child struggles with a word or misreads a word that alters meaning (for example, *horse* for *house*). These notes will give you something to come back to later (see Chapter 3 for a more in-depth discussion of the topic).

Working with a Small Group over Time

In this setting you will be working with your partner and a few other students. Consult with the host teacher to select group members who may have common interests and who may work well together. This small group may represent several levels of ability, and that should be viewed as a positive factor. Clearly this setting will bring children with diverse talents and needs together. Allow children to emerge as leaders where they have talents. You may find that your reading partner works well in a small group. In fact, you will likely discover that you learn a great deal from the interaction that occurs among children. These meetings with your reading partner as a member of a small group may provide you with the insight needed to focus some instruction during your one-on-one time. For example, members of the small group may demonstrate a strategy that you and your partner could borrow.

The small group setting provides an opportunity for you to see your partner employ strategies, observe others, or try out new strategies. You may find it useful to participate with your partner in a literature circle or to assist a small group through the process of an inquiry project, or the production of a play.

Literature Circles. If the idea of a literature circle is new to you it may be helpful to think about a book group you've participated in as an adult or to think about the book club featured on Oprah Winfrey's popular talk show. In each case a small group of people comes together because of common interest in the topic, admiration for the work of a particular author, or shared interest in the specific title or genre selected. These folks do not come together because they have similar scores on a test or show similar deficits in some particular skill. Instead, it is shared interest and common enthusiasm that brings them together. When folks gather for these "book clubs" the selection of a book is usually agreed upon by the members of the group and not imposed by someone else. Typically, there's a standard meeting time and place, and the group agrees upon the amount of time to be devoted to the book. If the group plans to meet prior to reading the whole book, they would agree to reading a specified amount of text for each meeting. The focus of each meeting is to share insights and confusions. The group gathers to discuss what they've connected with and made sense of. They also share what troubles or puzzles them. The discussion builds around these connections and confusions and may extend interpretations of the text. In essence, the group dynamics expands on the third view of reading (see page 5 in the Introduction). Here the insight and understanding gained by the reader rests not only with what the individual brings to the text because in this setting, the reader has the ideas, experiences, and language of the other members of the group to draw upon as well. In the literature circle, then, the interplay between reader and writer enlarges now to an interaction between readers and writer and *among readers* as well.

Also of note is the fact that when folks come together in these settings, there is usually no "quizzing" to see if all the members are prepared for the meeting. When questions are asked, they are asked out of genuine interest in the answers and opinions of others or from a true need to know. In short, this process emphasizes meaning, sharing ideas, broadening insights, and reducing confusions. It isn't about searching the page to find the "right" answer to someone else's questions.

The idea behind literature circles in the classroom is to provide that same opportunity for sharing perspectives, for making meaning, and reading for understanding. The intent is to allow children to bring their insights and interpretations and confusions to a group of their peers, who have interest in the same text. This is important for several reasons:

- children learn that comprehension is more than giving the "right" answer to someone else's questions
- children learn that comprehension is more a process of making sense of what is read than a process of finding the answer on the page
- children learn that sharing differing perspectives broadens the views of everyone and deepens the insights of all who participate
- children learn to read with an open mind seeking broader points of view, questioning the ideas of the writer, seeking to make sense of what is read, and to go beyond the details on the page
- children learn to value their own ideas and to respect the views of others even if they are different from their own.

As with any other strategy you work with in the classroom, it is always wise to begin by consulting with the teacher to seek suggestions and feedback as you make plans. Let the teacher be your guide and primary resource. Remember, your work should support and extend the foundation being built in that classroom. The person with the deepest insight into that foundation and with the greatest knowledge of the children there is the classroom teacher. If you are working in a program outside the school setting, your program coordinator would assume this role.

So you may be wondering just what you would do as the adult in this setting. Let's say you are working with a student in the third grade and the teacher suggests that you work with the child and a small group in a literature circle. First, consult the teacher for suggestions to identify appropriate books. You should also talk with the child to find out her interests and whether she has favorite authors or favorite types of stories. Armed with that information consult the librarian/media specialist in the school and bring three or four choices to the child. Give the child a brief "advertisement" for each book and have her identify her first and second choices. Now, your task is to locate enough copies of the book for each student who will be joining the group. In some cases, the teacher may prefer to establish the groups and identify the titles to be selected. If not, you would consult with the teacher to determine which children might be considered for joining your group. Then, you and your partner would present the selection as an invitation for three or four other children to join you in a literature circle with the selected book.

In many classrooms, literature circles will be a standard part of the reading program. In that case, you would simply join the circle your partner has selected. How these are established is determined by the classroom teacher and the children. However, children are typically given several options and join a circle on the basis of their interest in the book or author. As with adults, membership in a literature circle is not generally determined by a test score or skill deficit.

When the circle meets the first time, the group will need to agree upon meeting times, the amount to have read for each meeting, and a final date for having the book finished. Peterson and Eeds (1990) suggest using a literature study contract, which could look something like this.

Literature Study Contract

Name_____   Date_____

Title _____

Author_____

I agree to read this book by _____.

This book has a total of _____ pages. I will pace myself according to the schedule below.

Monday   _____ pages

Tuesday   _____ pages

Wednesday   _____ pages

Thursday   _____ pages

Friday   _____ pages

Saturday   _____ pages

Sunday   _____ pages

I will be prepared for meeting with my circle on _____.

Student's signature_____

Tutor's signature_____

Teacher's signature _____

Parent's signature _____

From Grand Conversations: Literature Groups in Action. *Reprinted with permission.*

Once the literature circle is formed and the limits have been set, you may play several roles. Your primary role, though, is to support your reading partner. You may listen to him read in between meetings of the circle. You may read with him or to him. You may take a copy of the book home and read it on tape so that he can use a "walkman" with a headset to listen and follow along. You may be reading the same pages at the same time, serving as a sounding board for his ideas, insights, and confusions to build confidence for his full participation in the circle. In short, you provide the level of support needed to allow the child to participate in the conversation with his peers. The type of support will differ from book to book depending upon the content, language, writing style, the child's familiarity with the topic, and his level of comfort with the text.

When the circle meets remember the purpose of the process is not to quiz the members to see if they have read. Instead, you and the children may begin by sharing your general impressions, talking through connections made to other texts (books, poems, songs, movies, etc.), sharing personal connections with the text, talking through confusions or things that made you wonder, and sharing observations or things you noted as a reader. Remember, one goal is to enrich and deepen the readers' understandings and insights. Peterson and Eeds (1990) remind us that "[w]hen a topic surfaces that commands the group's interest and has a potential for altering perception, the talk shifts from sharing to dialogue. Through dialogue, the group . . . works to disclose meaning, thereby potentially expanding the meaning of the work for all participants. . . . Through the collaborative work of the group, time is spent contemplating meaning, and digesting it. Group members help each other begin to see where previously they may have only looked. Our job . . . is to help with this seeing" (p. 13).

In many classrooms, the members of literature circles also keep reading response logs. Again, it is wise to check with your host teacher to determine the extent to which response logs are used. Basically, the log is a place for the reader to record general impressions, to note connections to other texts and to personal experiences, and to write through confusions and noticings. The log could be just a blank notebook or may take a more structured format. A possible structure could include any or all of the following:

- brief retelling
- observations and insights
- connections to other texts
- connections to personal experience
- confusions

The retelling allows readers an opportunity to express the essence of the story in their own words. The observations might focus on details in the story, the writer's choice of words, the use of a repeated phrase throughout the book. The connections to other texts invite readers to note how the story reminds them of other books, stories, poems, movies, TV shows, music, etc. The point is to note how knowledge of various texts makes it easier to make meaning of new texts and to help readers realize that some themes cut across the human experience. The connections to personal experience help readers to bring meaning to the text in order to make sense of the text. Recognizing our personal experiences in the stories of others can be very validating. The confusions might include misunderstandings, a need for more information, clarification of vocabulary, or just curiosity about the plot or why the author chose to write the story as it is.

The writing that readers do in the response logs can be the springboard into the conversations that take place in the literature circles. In short, the whole process is one of read, write, and talk. Each component is of great significance and contributes to the making of meaning. You might say this process is view three of reading (see Introduction) in action. Clearly, the readers must rely upon all their skills and strategies, making use of all available cues both on the page and in the mind. And most important, the goal—the end result is making sense of what is read.

Locating Books and Other Material for Literature Circles, Author Studies, Genre Studies, or Topic Studies. If you want to help between your tutoring sessions you could assist the teacher in locating texts for literature circles, author studies, genre studies, and topic studies. You may locate and collect books by an author (e.g., titles by Eric Carle, by Bill Martin Jr., and by others) or books about the same topic (e.g., titles about losing a tooth, about moving to a new town, etc.). In this way, you will help to continue the literature circles within the classroom by locating books for your partner and other groups. Your reading partner will benefit from continued participation in literature study. Reading with a small group with a common interest in a title, author, genre, or topic allows your partner to observe the strategies and connections of other readers in the class. In a classroom where a more traditional view of reading is practiced, the developing reader rarely has the opportunity to participate in reading with more proficient readers. Therefore, the strategies most often observed are those of the less proficient readers in the class. It is no wonder that these students tend to have limited skills and strategies. To encourage further participation, it might benefit your partner, as well as others in the class, if you locate sets of books that might be used by the children between your visits. Consult with your host teacher to determine the authors, titles, topics, and genres that might be most appropriate. You can often find enough copies by borrowing from classroom collections in your host school. You may also want to check the school and local libraries. And don't forget to consult the librarians for guidance in using technology that may make the search more fruitful. If you plan ahead, you may find that children have copies to loan and that friends of yours may have copies stored away in their own children's book collections. Suggest any you find particularly interesting yourself. Some possibilities are also included in the appendix.

Inquiry Project. In many classrooms children participate in a process of inquiring about a topic of intense interest or significance. The process could include identifying the topic; discussing and recording what is already known or believed to be true; generating questions for research; locating resources (print and nonprint); reading, viewing, listening, and note taking; reviewing new information and generating more specific questions; more reading, viewing, note taking; synthesizing the information and deciding how to share the findings. You can help your partner or group talk through the topic and assist with recording what is known. Some teachers do this with a web, some prefer a K-W-L chart. The -K- is the heading for the column where you record what is **K**nown. The -W- heads the column for what we **W**ant to know and the -L- heads the column for what was **L**earned.

Sample web: teaching about polar bears

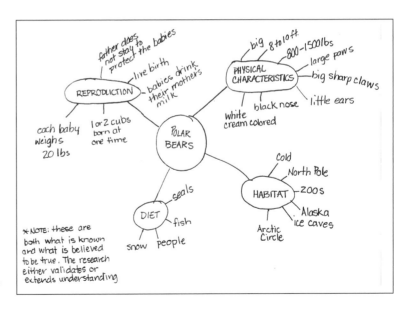

As you and the child(ren) get the known recorded, move on to the questions that will guide your search for resources and new information. You should note that initially the questions are likely to be very simple. Remember that the children may need the opportunity to locate a few resources and gather a bit of information before they have enough information to ask more in-depth questions. You may find it helpful to cluster the questions around categories. For example, if the topic is polar bears, the questions might easily cluster around these categories—*physical*

K	W	L
• polar bears are big • they are white • they live in cold places • babies are only 1-2 pounds at birth	• what do they eat • how much do they weigh • what do they live in • does the father help raise the cubs	the results of research are recorded here. You would also note whether you validate or extend what you have in the Known column

CATEGORIES	PREDICTIONS	FINDINGS
HABITAT	Arctic Circle North Pole Alaska Zoos	In this column indicate whether the prediction is correct. If not, record the finding along with the source. Categories can be used to learn about using an index, table of content or other reference tools.
DIET	Fish Seals people snow	
PHYSICAL CHARACTERISTICS	big 8-10 ft. tall 800 - 1500 pounds white, creamy color black nose little ears	

Sample K-W-L chart

characteristics, habitat, diet, care, and feeding of the young.* Having the questions and categories can help with locating resources. You could easily use this opportunity to demonstrate the function of the table of contents, the glossary, the appendix, the card catalog, and any technology the library may have to aid in the search for material. For example, as you and your partner begin the search for information, help your partner clearly identify the questions. Next, you may review the table of contents for each of your print resources and compare the entries with each of your questions. As you find a match, place the question number on a sticky note and affix the note on the corresponding page in that resource. This will help your partner learn how to locate information using reference skills and to reduce the amount of time needed.

The appendix can also be used to make your partner's use of resources more efficient. For example, the categories from the polar bear web are key headings for information. You and your partner could use sticky notes (perhaps a different color this time) to list each heading. Then turn to the index in your first resource to search for the category—*habitat.* On the sticky note, jot down the corresponding page numbers. Repeat this process for each resource and each heading. In doing this with your partner, you demonstrate how readers make efficient use of resources. The appendixes in books can be useful in similar ways, and the glossary can be used to help your partner define unfamiliar terms and to discover other key terms that may prove useful in the quest for information.

The categories from the web can be also useful for organizing notes and may become headings in the final product if the child(ren) should decide to write a summary of the findings. Remember that inquiry, the search for information and insight, tends to feed itself. Each cycle of this process will lead to greater insight, better questions, more skill with identifying and locating resources and more in-depth note taking, and more informed readers and writers. Clearly, this will require focused reading and writing and is a process that will not be limited to one subject. These experiences also enable you to see the range of strategies and skills employed in the classroom. That insight can only broaden the possibilities for you and your partner.

Producing a Play. Most of us can remember being part of a school play during those elementary grades. You may remember the part you played or the butterflies in your stomach when the curtains were parted and the auditorium was filled with more faces than you'd ever stood before. What you may not remember is the amount of focused reading you did to learn your part and to know the parts of others well enough to know when you should act or speak. Working together with your partner alone or with a small group to produce a play can be a rewarding experience for all involved. You may begin with a familiar story and work together to write a script. Then there are parts to read and reread through many rehearsals before the performance is ready for an audience. The play may be presented through the use of puppets with your partner and friends reading the parts of different voices. In any case, the process is clearly one that involves the use of many practical reading strategies and skills.

Working with an Individual Child over Time

Working with one child over an extended period of time, such as one school year, can be among the most rewarding experiences you'll have. The one-to-one setting enables you to gain intense knowledge of the child's reading habits, strengths, strategies, interests, and limitations. When working with one child over time you soon find that you visit libraries with your partner in mind. You find yourself running across a new title or an old favorite saying, "I should check this out, it would be perfect for our next meeting." It is thrilling to make progress as a team, to see your partner gain confidence and competence as a literate being.

Helpful Materials

Regardless of the setting you find yourself working in there are certain materials and strategies you will want to employ. What follows is a listing of suggested materials and strategies with a brief description.

IN THIS SECTION ➤

- *Predictable books*
- *I Can Read books*
- *Picture books*
- *Alphabet (ABC) books*

Predictable Books

What Are They?

Predictable books are structured in ways that enable the reader to predict the text, based on the structures or patterns employed. Books such as *Brown Bear, Brown Bear, What Do You See?*, *The Hungry Caterpillar*, *Big Fat Hen*, and *The Little Old Lady Who Swallowed a Fly* are examples of predictable books.

Brown Bear, Brown Bear uses art and a language pattern to make the print more accessible for the young reader. "Brown Bear, Brown Bear what do you see?" The response always names the next animal and color to appear on the following page, "I see a red bird looking at

From Brown Bear, Brown Bear, What Do You See? *Reprinted with permission.*

me." This is followed by "Red Bird, Red Bird, What do you see?" and the pattern continues.

The Hungry Caterpillar uses a combination of art, a cultural sequence (days of the week), and number. "On Monday he ate through one . . . , On Tuesday he ate through two . . ."

Big Fat Hen uses a familiar nursery rhyme. "1, 2, buckle my shoe. 3, 4 shut the door. . . . "

The Little Old Lady Who Swallowed a Fly uses a cumulative, repetitive pattern as in *The House That Jack Built*.

Why Are They Helpful?

Predictable books provide support for the young or struggling reader. That element of repeated words or phrases, a cumulative repetitive pattern, the use of cultural sequences like days of the week or months of the year or numbers or alphabetical order, reduces the number of cues the child must decode. Predictable books provide a sense of security, a sense of knowing what to expect.

How Would You Use Them?

With the least developed readers I would begin by reading the book with the child encouraging him or her to chime in whenever possible. After a few readings, many children will begin to explore the patterns on their own and work to make sense of the text with a little guidance. As you read together, slowly move your finger under the words. As you read *Brown Bear, Brown Bear, What Do You See?* you might occasionally ask "Can you show me where it says, 'What do you see?'" This directs the child's attention to the fact that the print indeed carries the story, that the printed word has a spoken word to accompany it, that the print moves from left to right and top to bottom on the page, and that there are boundaries between each printed word.

I Can Read Books

What Are They?

I Can Read books are usually very short books with a simple story and only a few characters. These are characterized by simple story lines, a generous use of white space and large, clear print. Usually, there are very few lines on each page, and simple illustrations are used to enhance the language. I Can Read books usually have very short chapters. Some are a little larger, but they have the appearance of "big kid" books even though there are usually far fewer pages. Some have short segments that could be viewed as chapters. However, there are many I Can Read books that present the story as a whole (without chapters or segments). Books such as *Titch, And I Mean it Stanley,* and the *Frog and Toad* stories are examples.

For a more complete listing of books in this category see the appendix.

Why Are They Helpful?

I Can Read books provide both confidence and early independence while they serve as the important step between materials like

Listen, Stanley.
I know you are there.
I know you are
in back of the fence.

7

But I don't care, Stanley.
I don't want to play with you.
I don't want to talk to you.

8

You stay there, Stanley.
Stay in back of the fence.
I don't care.

9

From And I Mean It, Stanley. *Reprinted with permission.*

predictable books and the first independent chapter books. In many ways I Can Read books serve as the stepping stones to independent reading behaviors.

How Would You Use Them?

I Can Read books are appropriate for use with children who demonstrate some independent reading strategies. You read them to your reading partner. You might partner-read, where you read one page or paragraph and the child reads the next, taking turns until the story is complete. You ask the child to read the story for you or to read it silently. Following the reading, regardless of the strategy you select, you would have the child retell the story. "So what's going on in this story?"

The Letter

Toad was sitting on his front porch.
Frog came along and said,
"What is the matter, Toad?
You are looking sad."

53

"Yes," said Toad.
This is my sad time of day.
It is the time
when I wait for the mail to come.
It always makes me very unhappy."
"Why is that?" asked Frog.
"Because I never get any mail,"
said Toad.

54

"Not ever?" asked Frog.
"No, never," said Toad.
"No one has ever sent me a letter.
Every day my mailbox is empty.
That is why waiting for the mail
is a sad time for me."
Frog and Toad sat on the porch,
feeiling sad together.

55

From Frog and Toad Are Friends. *Reprinted with permission.*

"What is this story all about?" Then, share your favorite part and ask your partner to do the same. "I like this section here on page ___, where Frog and Toad decide to eat the cookies anyway. That reminds me of myself and my friend Shirley. We can talk ourselves into eating candy anytime. What was your favorite part?" Here you not only demonstrate the idea of having a favorite part, you also show how to articulate your rationale.

Picture Books

What Are They?

Picture books are stories for young readers that have both text and illustrations. Usually the illustrations are large and play an important role in communicating the story. The language in picture books should be able to carry the story while the art should enrich and enhance the detail and texture of the overall effect. Picture books are organized in 32-page spreads, and each illustration is paired with a specific segment of the text. There may be pages with art only, which serves to fill some details or perhaps enhance the language from previous pages. Where predictable books are designed for independent reading, the picture book story may be one the child can read independently or one that is intended for reading aloud. Though many folks think of picture books for children in the four- to eight-year-old range, these books can strike a chord with readers from birth to death. Examples of picture books include *Wilfrid McDonald Gordon Partridge, All the Places to Love, The Polar Express, The Library Dragon, My Great Aunt Arizona, Water Dance,* and *The Sunsets of Miss Olivia Wiggins.* For a more detailed list see the appendix.

These titles represent a range of complexity in language and story, and each would be useful in working with a child. It is important to remember that picture books do cover a range of topics and issues. Picture books may be written in simple and sparse language or in more compex sentence patterns using rich descriptive language. Read the stories before meeting with your partner and select those you plan to read aloud, determine which ones you plan to read with the child, and have some for the child to select for independent reading.

Why Are They Helpful?

Picture books are essential to the reading/writing lives of children. Picture books typically have well-crafted language along with engaging

She held me up in the open window
So that what I heard first was the wind.
What I saw first were all the places to love:
The valley,
The river falling down over rocks,
The hilltop where the blueberries grew.

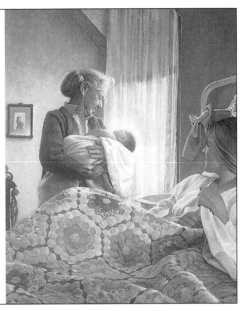

From All the Places to Love. *Reprinted with permission.*

art that provides additional support to the reader. The presence of both artfully crafted language and detailed art provides the young reader with cues for constructing meaning. This is particularly significant when children are discovering the meanings of words they have not heard and have not encountered before. Often, the additional support provided by the illustrations enables the child to make sense of the unfamiliar language. At times, the illustrations also serve the adult well. I have found the illustrations very useful when reading aloud to children, particularly when types of dwellings, articles of clothing, an

From The Sunsets of Miss Olivia Wiggins.
Reprinted with permission.

She remembered an afternoon not so long ago. Her house was filled with cousins, nieces and nephews, her children, grandchildren and great-grandchildren. It was the last birthday she had at home. After the celebration, each one came by to say happy birthday and give her a hug before leaving. All but Angel. She and Angel sat chatting on the porch swing, and she took Angel's hand. The chains on the swing creaked responses to crickets and frogs as the sun cast long shadows across the yard. Angel squeezed her hand and said, "Happy birthday, Momma. I love you." Then she saw one of the last rays of sun catch Angel from behind and wrap her in a golden halo.

unfamiliar animal, modes of transportation, and the like are introduced. I find it helpful to reread the sentence or paragraph and refer the child to the art. "Let's look at the illustration here and see if the artist offers us any help on that one?" Picture books are useful as they demonstrate the range of possibilities for story; they exist as examples of the interdependence of language and art, and they demonstrate the range of genres available (memoir, biography, poetry, fiction, fantasy, humor, etc.) for children as readers and as writers.

How Would You Use Them?

As mentioned above, picture books have a wide variety of uses. You might read them aloud. In that case your purpose might be to expose your partner to beautiful language or well-crafted writing in telling a story. You might use them to introduce a concept, extend an idea or deepen an understanding tied to a content area such as history, science, or math. You might study how writers write. For example, you and your reading partner might look at the opening lines of several different books. You might read them to note the significance of place or the setting, to the development of story. Perhaps you and your partner explore a topic from more than one perspective. In addition to these possibilities, picture books typically can be read in one sitting, which allows a sense of completion and success for a young or struggling reader.

Alphabet (ABC) Books

What Are They?

ABC books are organized around a presentation of the alphabet. Usually, these books take a concept and present it through a series of illustrations, words, phrases, or sentences in which each page features one letter. *Tomorrow's Alphabet, Handmade Alphabet,* and *Alphabet City,* are examples of ABC books.

See the appendix for a more complete list. You could also consult your local or school librarian for a list of ABC books available. Your host teacher or coordinator may also have some in the classroom.

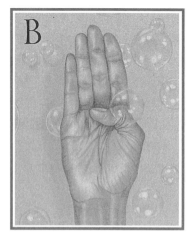

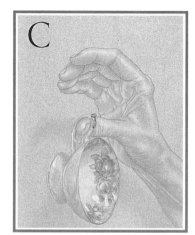

Left: From Tomorrow's Alphabet. *Reprinted with permission.*

Right: From The Handmade Alphabet. *Reprinted with permission.*

Why Are They Helpful?

ABC books present a familiar cultural sequence that makes the text somewhat more predictable. In addition, these books are useful for repeated exposure to the alphabet and alphabetical order, exploring a variety of concepts, or expanding vocabulary.

How Would You Use Them?

You could use ABC books to explore the uses of alphabetical order, classifying, categorizing, initial sounds. You could read several and select a topic (e.g., cars, kids in the second grade, names of towns, fruits, vegetables, stores, street names, NFL/NBA/college teams, insects, mammals, reptiles, on and on and on) and create your own.

The process of producing your own ABC book might involve searching through magazines, class lists, picture files, and such. It might involve having a small group come together for a brainstorming session. The book you and your partner produce may have only the capital letter and the name of the item featured. It could include illustrations, a word or phrase, a sentence or description. It could be a fact collection or presented in rhyme. There are numerous possibilities; just present the idea to your partner and have fun. You'll be surprised by the research, reading, and writing necessary to create a satisfactory product.

Helpful Strategies

The following strategies can be very helpful as you look for ways to utilize the materials described above. As you read, keep the needs of your student in mind and select those strategies and materials that you believe will best match the strengths, interests, and needs of your partner. It is always wise to consult your host teacher or project coordinator when in doubt.

Language Experience Approach

The Language Experience Approach (LEA) has been widely used as an effective strategy for demonstrating the connections between

<< IN THIS SECTION

- *Language experience approach*
- *Cloze procedure*
- *Skimming and scanning*
- *Echo reading*
- *Choral reading*
- *Reader's theater*
- *Poetry performance*
- *Rhymes to prose*
- *Story to script*
- *The talking book*

experience, thought, spoken language, and written language. You begin with something concrete, say baking cookies or making fresh lemonade. The child or group and you would talk through the event as it happens. You might make notes as you go or you may wait until afterwards before writing anything. After the cookies are baked and have been eaten, you initiate a discussion to review the ingredients, the recipe, the process. Encourage the child or group to add details about how the cookies smelled as they were baking, how the dough felt in their hands, how the cookies tasted. Encourage the children to make connections to their own memories. The important thing here is to enjoy the experience and to generate functional uses of language. The talk centers around thinking in logical sequences, remembering the order of ingredients and the steps in the process. The talk provides opportunities for the child or group to use language to express perceptions, to describe, to sequence, to make connections. As the adult in the group, you can participate in the conversation and then move toward capturing a written account of the event.

Your purpose here is to demonstrate how all that talk, all those pieces of information, all those details and images can be organized for a story (a narrative account) or a list of ingredients, or a recipe with step-by-step directions for a classroom with only a small toaster oven, or as a critique of the cookies. Here you might present the possibilities for the form the written account might take. Then talk with the child or group to decide what information might be needed to generate that written account. You could invite the child to write or you could serve as the scribe yourself and write a list of information to be included. Next, talk through the sequence of the information and note what should be used in which order. Then generate a beginning and take down a written account. While doing all this, remember that your primary purpose here is to generate a text to read. All the while, you are demonstrating and the child or group is participating in the process of moving from lived experience to print. The process of LEA, adapted from Roach Van Allen's well-known work (1976) on the subject, can be summarized as follows:

What I can do, I can think about
What I can think about, I can talk about
What I can talk about, I can write
What I can write, I can read

The basic idea, then, is that you take common experiences and talk them through. Once the experience is complete and the text has been generated, you read through the account to verify events and allow individuals to revise as needed. You can point out the conventions of print (capital letters, spelling, punctuation, letter formation, spacing) as you and the children move through the text. Always make these connections in meaningful ways. For example, think aloud as you write and tell the child(ren) what you are doing. "We'll need to use quotation marks here to show that Aubrey is saying this." "What kind of punctuation mark should we use here to show our readers that we were excited about those cookies?" You might also point to connections between words. For example, "Did you notice that *William* and *Winnie* and *wishing* all begin with the same letter? That's right, these words begin with W, and listen as we read them. Did you notice how your mouth moves as you begin to say each of these words?" Calling attention to those letters and sounds that are used in several places throughout the text is an easy way to have young readers begin to look for such connections on their own. And remember, no matter how good we are as tutors, our purpose is to develop readers and writers who can function without us. Therefore, right from the start, get the children to write their own accounts of the events you are using to generate these small group stories. Clearly, each child will have similar details in the personal accounts, and these can be the starting point for the group account.

LEA is very successful because the meaning is understood in that the text is about an event in the reader's life. In addition, the text is the reader's language.

Cloze Procedure

The cloze procedure involves presenting a reader with a text that has words deleted on a systematic basis, every fifth word for example. The reader's task is to use the context cues to read the text. The cloze procedure has been modified in many ways over the years. However, the basic idea is that you begin with a reading selection. I always prefer to have a complete piece, that is, a whole story or poem. Usually these are relatively short selections. Next you type the selection leaving a blank in the place of every nth (5th, 10th, etc.) word. The child would be asked to read the selection and orally insert a word that would make sense in the blank. Here the point is to develop the reader's ability to use semantic (meaning) cues and syntactic (grammatical) cues to make sense of unknown words. The procedure has been modified many times to fit the various needs of different students. For example, you might blank out only adjectives, or only verbs, or delete every fifth word while leaving the first letter of the word intact. How you opt to employ this strategy should be determined by your partner's strengths and needs. Here again, it would be wise to seek input from your host teacher or program coordinator.

An example of a cloze exercise with every fifth word deleted follows:

The Big Storm

Last Thursday I was _____ my bike home from _____ when I got caught _____ the big storm. I _____ something was going to _____ when I noticed the _____ moving faster and faster. _____ sky grew darker and _____. It was only 3:15 _____ already it looked like _____ Then came the blinding _____ just across the ball _____ and crashing boom that _____ and rattled the windows _____ the gym. Faster than _____ could pedal the rain _____ down in buckets. I _____ soaked by the time _____ reached the gym. I _____ I was lucky that _____ hadn't gotten farther. I _____ have been trapped in _____ storm with no place _____ go.

Sample cloze exercise

Below is the same cloze exercise with initial sounds left in place for each deleted word.

The Big Storm

Last Thursday I was r_____ my bike home from sch_____ when I got caught i_____ the big storm. I kn_____ something was going to h_____ when I noticed the c_____ moving faster and faster. Th_____ sky grew darker and d_____. It was only 3:15 a_____ already it looked like d_____. Then came the blinding fl_____ just across the ball f_____ and crashing boom that e_____ and rattled the windows o_____ the gym. Faster than I_____ could pedal the rain c_____ down in buckets. I w_____ soaked by the time I_____ reached the gym. I g_____ I was lucky that I_____ hadn't gotten farther. I w_____ have been trapped in th_____ storm with no place t_____ go.

Here is the full passage. Read through to see how close you were.

The Big Storm

Last Thursday I was riding my bike home from school when I got caught in the big storm. I knew something was going to happen when I noticed the clouds moving faster and faster. The sky grew darker and darker. It was only 3:15 and already it looked like dusk. Then came the blinding flash just across the ball field and crashing boom that echoed and rattled the windows on the gym. Faster than I could pedal the rain came down in buckets. I was soaked by the time I reached the gym. I guess I was lucky that I hadn't gotten further. I would have been trapped in the storm with no place to go.

Well, if you read through the three passages you probably found that as a reader, you rely quite heavily upon your experiences and your knowledge of language. And you may have noticed that context cues found in the text (meaning and grammar) helped as well. Clearly, this demonstrates that readers make use of world knowledge and word knowledge, that reading is (as described in view three in the Introduction) a complex act involving an array of strategies and skills working together in the meaning making mind of a reader.

You may also find it beneficial to modify this strategy as an oral cloze procedure. Here you would read a text aloud and delete (or pause before) selected words and wait for your partner to supply the word. This experience requires your partner to listen and to make use of meaning and language cues as well. This process provides opportunities for your partner to engage in the same kind of thinking that will be required later when reading the text independently.

Skimming and Scanning

These are not strategies used frequently by very young readers. However, you may be working with an eight- to nine-year-old who is having difficulty with textbook material. In many schools the curriculum begins to be more subject-specific in the third and fourth grade. In some schools there are textbooks for each subject (health, social studies, science). To avoid being bogged down, your partner may benefit from learning to skim chapter headings, topic sentences, charts, tables, and graphs. You may also find it useful to demonstrate scanning for using glossaries, indexes, or tables of contents.

Skimming is a strategy usually used by readers who are interested in getting an overview of the story or information presented. To skim a selection the reader might read headings, the first two sentences in each paragraph, sentences containing bold or italicized words, and/or any charts, tables, or graphs presented. Again, the point here would be to gain an overview or the basic frame for the text. This would enable the reader to determine whether the text were appropriate to his or her interests, purposes, or needs. It is very much what we adults, as proficient readers, do when looking over books on gardening, woodworking, furniture refinishing, and other interests or hobbies. We use similar strategies when reviewing new titles on the bestseller list when we read the jacket and a paragraph here and there. Skimming can be a useful strategy for your partner to use when locating information for a project, when selecting a book to read, when reviewing material in a textbook, or when preparing to read textbook material.

Scanning is a similar strategy that readers use when searching for a specific piece of information such as the name of a city, a description, a definition, a telephone number or address. To scan for information the reader might use guide words as in dictionaries and telephone directories. The index or table of contents might be used. The reader may also quickly look through a chapter noticing only the headings and words in bold. Here, the purpose is not about gaining an overview or building some cumulative understanding of the whole. Instead, when scanning the reader is searching for a clue that will help to zero in on something more specific. This strategy is guided by a specific need for a particular piece of information. As adults, we use scanning frequently as we quickly look for phone numbers or an address, the correct spelling in a dictionary, and even when searching for a particular brand of cereal among the hundreds presented on the grocery aisle.

Scanning can be useful to your partner in searching for a specific detail to include in a story or report. Or when looking up the meaning or correct spelling of a word. Scanning greatly reduces the labor and time readers spend on such tasks.

Echo Reading

When reading with a young child you will find that with favorite books a child will tend to chime in on refrains, repeated lines or phrases, predictable sequences and the like. This natural tendency should be encouraged and can be extended to lead the child to independence. One way to do just that is through echo reading. To do this, you would select a piece that has high predictability or one that has been read several times and is a favorite of the child. Sit so that both you and the child can see the print clearly and so that the child can touch the page along with you. As you read, trail your finger along the line of print just under the words as they are being read. Don't point word by word; rather, keep the pace slow but expressive moving your finger in a slow and steady pace along with your voice. Encourage the child to chime in and to read along, to touch the page, and trail the print along with you. The process is similar to the day you removed the training wheels from your child's first bike. Both you and your child wanted that new-found freedom and independence, but your child also needed the security of having you there holding the seat, promising to not let go. As you ran along behind the bike, you removed your hand and watched your child ride alone. All the while you were an arm's length away at the ready if the bike should begin to wobble. Slowly you were able to just hold the bike and help the child get started, and you just stood there and watched; only your presence was needed for security. Before long the child was independently riding the bike. In many ways, echo reading is providing that sense of security and leadership. You set the pace, demonstrate the inflection and expression of proficient reading. The child joins in where there is a comfort zone and quietly fades out when that confidence wanes. As the child joins in more and more, your voice becomes less obvious, and the roles tend to reverse until the child is doing most, if not all, of the reading. As the child takes ownership of one book, begin others so that there are new books or stories the child is growing into as he takes control of older ones. Clearly, this is not the only strategy you will use. It will however, be one that will build confidence, fluency, and a growing sight vocabulary.

Choral Reading

As the term implies, choral reading is done with several voices in unison. When working with your partner this might be done with just the two of you or may include the voices of others in the class. Choral reading can be both useful and pleasant with the right material. Poems, rhymes, chants often take on a different effect when read in unison by many voices. Some stories, poems, plays, and songs have parts where one voice is clearly speaking and other parts where several voices seem to be called for. In those situations you might read the single voice and you and your partners together (along with others if appropriate) might read the refrains or segments for many voices. You may find that entire texts work well when read together. In any case, choral reading provides the opportunity for young readers to hear the flow and rhythm of written language read aloud. It also provides a safe zone for joining in a chorus of voices. The significance of this is that no one child is singled out, and in the places where one child may struggle, another is likely to keep the flow moving. This provides the effect of an uninterrupted reading, allowing each child to join in where she can. As with echo reading, choral reading is a strategy you will find helpful for building confidence, word-recognition, and fluency. Since neither of these strategies directly involves a focus on comprehension, you may want to have the child retell the story, relate the song, poem, or story to life events or to other stories. This would, of course, not be necessary each time the piece is revisited. Just understand that your purpose then would be to enjoy the language and build confidence and competence. See the appendix for suggested texts for choral reading.

Reader's Theater

If you've ever listened to a recording of the old radio theater productions you have some idea of what a reader's theater is about. Here, the players have no actions. Instead the presentation is all in the voices of readers. The simplest of reader's theater productions would involve a script and a reader or readers. You and your partner could take almost any story and work together to create a script for the story. Usually there would be a narrator who reads the connecting text to set up the scenes and then there would be one voice for each character in the story. Clearly, you could involve as many readers as you have characters or you and your partner could divide the parts among yourselves. Although prepared scripts are available for many stories, think of the tremendous opportunities for reading and rereading a story to identify all the characters and to separate the script from the narration. Think of the opportunities for talk and writing to generate the script. If the story were one of intense interest to the reader there could be powerful opportunities for literacy development. Once the script has been prepared you will need several rehearsals and then a performance. The performance could be live, in which case you and your partner (and other readers if you feel it's necessary) would need nothing more than your scripts, chairs or stools, and an audience. Or you could record your performance, creating a tape that could be played for an audience much like an old radio theater. In this case you may want to work in a few sound effects.

Poetry Performance

Many poems are filled with action and emotion and lend themselves to physical and vocal performance. Following a procedure similar to the one described for reader's theater, you and your partner could read through poetry collections to select those you believe will be most appropriate for performing. The performance, then, may be a dramatic reading; a reading paired with interpretative actions, music, rhythms, or dance. Clearly, a performance of any written work requires the reader to attend to print and ideas; to understand, interpret and act on ideas.

Rhymes to Prose

A friend of mine, Theresa Brown, now retired from years of teaching kindergarten used to fascinate her five-year-olds with nursery rhymes. Many of her children came to school knowing the rhymes from having heard them so many times at home. Other children were being exposed for the first time. Theresa had the rhymes written out on large chart sheets and would begin the week with a new rhyme. To move from rhyme to prose, you and your partner would review the rhyme, reading through it together a few times. As you do, discuss the characters and events. Point out the use of conventions (capital letters, punctuation, line breaks, etc.) and talk about how the rhyme might be made into a story. Next, you would talk about a good opening line for the prose version ("Once upon a time . . . ," "Once there was . . . ," "One night long ago . . . ," "On a rainy Thursday afternoon . . ."). It is good to read the opening lines in several favorite stories for ideas. Mrs. Brown found that many children would limit their suggestions to the standard, "Once upon a time," until she began pointing out the different ways that stories begin. Once you and your partner have agreed upon a good opening, you should work together to develop the characters, the setting, and the plot. This is easy to do as you review the rhyme together just ask questions such as, Who is the rhyme about? What can you tell me about this person or these people? Where is this all happening? What time of day do you suppose it is? What season of the year might it be? What are these folks doing in the rhyme? Did they have a problem or face an obstacle? What did our character(s) do about that? How did that work out? Then talk about ways to end the story and give a sense of conclusion. Here again you might visit the endings of favorite stories. As you talk through all this, you and your

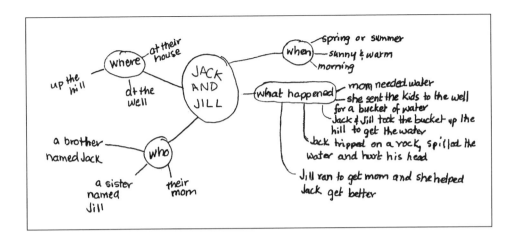

Moving from rhyme to prose. Source: This illustration by Theresa M. Brown and Lester L. Laminack originally appeared in Early Years K–8 (January 1988).

partner would be keeping notes, making a web, creating lists, making an outline or some other system for capturing your ideas.

At this point, the two of you would talk out the story and write the draft. Read through the draft and discuss word choices and test the language for its ability to elicit images. Read the story aloud noting the effect of the punctuation and other conventions used. Make changes as necessary to achieve the desired phrasing. Listen to a reading of the rhyme now and then a reading of the story version. Does it sound like story language? When you and your partner are satisfied you might print out the story in segments and illustrate each one to make a book for the class. This could be done with most poems, rhymes, and chants, and it works particularly well with the traditional nursery rhymes.

Story to Script

Following the example of moving from rhyme to prose, you and your partner could easily take traditional tales (e.g., *Little Red Riding Hood, Goldilocks and the Three Bears, The Three Billy Goats Gruff*) and generate a script for a short play. The play could involve other students in the class as characters. It could be produced as a puppet show, where you and your partner are the voices, or it might be produced as a reader's theater. Here your basic procedure would be very similar to the rhyme-to-prose strategy. The primary difference is in determining the stage directions and separating the narration from the script.

The Talking Book

When my son, Zachary, was about four or five, we began what we called our talking book. The book is a large (about 9" × 12") blank book purchased at a local bookstore. We used the book to "talk" to each other so Mom wouldn't know what we were saying. Actually, it was my way of encouraging Zachary to use reading and writing, to act on his developing knowledge of how written language worked. At times I had to read my message to him. At times it was necessary for him to read his message to me. We worked together. In this strategy several important things happen at once. First, the child is being given a powerful message, "I believe you are a reader and a writer." Second, there is a caring and interested and non-threatening audience. Third, there is ready and able support for the developing reader/writer. Last, and definitely not least, there is the ongoing demonstration of the conventional use of written language for a powerful purpose. This strategy also provides an exciting documentation of growth and development over time.

◆ CHAPTER 2 ◆

Getting Started

The First Meeting

So you're ready for your first day in the school as a reading volunteer. Where do you start? Here are a few suggestions you might consider. First, ease your way into the routine of the classroom. Think about spending your first visit or two getting a feel for the routine in the classroom. Find out how the day unfolds for the class and your partner. You might begin by sharing a favorite story or reading aloud. Before you begin working one-on-one with your partner let the children get acquainted with you and see you as a part of the learning community. During the time you are a volunteer, try to be a part of the classroom whenever you can. This will accomplish at least two goals. One, you'll be seen as a non-threatening visitor who shares stories and delightful books. This is significant because you may work with small groups from time to time, and all the children need to be comfortable with

≺ IN THIS SECTION

- *Language is social*
- *Literacy is language*
- *Literacy develops over time*
- *Children bring a wealth of knowledge to school*
- *Instruction needs to be provided in a supportive environment*
- *Reading materials should be authentic*
- *Reading is understanding*
- *Meaning and making sense must serve as the frame for considering skills*

your presence in the room. Two, you'll get the opportunity to see your partner interact with peers as a member of the class. This can give you insight about how your partner uses reading strategies and works in a group.

When you meet with your partner for the first time, take along some things that you know will spark interest. You might consider taking a shoe box with a few items that will help your partner get to know you. The box might contain a favorite book, a seashell from a trip to your favorite beach, a picture of your family, and a few other small items that allow you to introduce yourself. Invite the child to bring a box to introduce himself the next time. This time is well spent. The more you know about your partner, the better you are able to match your strategies with your partner's needs.

Your observations, interactions, and instruction will be guided by those principles you hold as truths about literacy and learning. This book provides strategies and suggestions guided by several basic principles. Included among these principles are the following.

Language Is Social

Language is the means by which we communicate ideas, feelings, needs, information to others. We speak to make ourselves known to others, to express our needs and our desires. We speak to gain information from others. We listen to receive information from others. Listening and speaking are means of communicating between or among two or more individuals. Language, then, is by its very nature a social activity. In fact, without a social network of speakers and listeners language would not be acquired.

Literacy Is Language

Literacy, the act of reading and writing, is a language activity. After all, what we read and write is language. What the writer puts on paper is language. What the reader deciphers is language. Clearly, there are differences between the writer's spoken and written accounts. However, it is clearly language that the writer uses to tell his or her story. One primary difference is the "code" used. In a spoken account the code is oral language and the audience receives the story through listening. The task of the audience is to "decode" the oral language. In a written account the code is written language and the audience receives the story through reading. The task of the audience is to "decode" the written language. For us to assume that the acts of reading and writing are anything less than a language activity is to deny the connections between reading, writing, listening, and speaking. Because these connections are present, we should build on the child's natural strengths with oral language when leading them to literate lives.

The child's natural tendencies can be the basis of your strategies to bring the child to the written word. You can bring out the child's natural tendencies to question the speaker when spoken words fail to make sense, to ask the meaning of a word used by a speaker, to ask the speaker to repeat an unclear or confusing phrase, to focus on listening to make sense, to latch onto an interesting or unusual spoken word. By encouraging all these natural tendencies you help bring the child to the written word.

As and you and your partner work with reading and writing it would be wise to "name" these natural tendencies as strategies for written languge. When reading, show the child how you "question" the writer when the print isn't making sense. Let your partner see you read on beyond to find meaning. Let him see you stop and reread to clarify. The point is to make that natural search for meaning an automatic strategy with reading.

Literacy Develops over Time

In that literacy is language and language develops over time, it stands to reason that literacy will not develop rapidly in a few short lessons. We know and accept that children come to spoken language over a period of time. Some more rapidly than others. Some with greater ease than others. But, it does take time. In fact, some speech and language experts contend that children should not be expected to master articulation of all speech sounds until the age of eight. That is not to say that many children will not do this earlier. Rather, it is to remind us that language is a developmental process involving many variables and that it is not a major concern if a six-year-old pronounces "rabbit" as "wabbit." Children move through a wealth of experiences between

their first babblings, sighs, and coos and their first words, their first two-
and three-word sentences, and then to more fully developed speech.
Adults tend to be patient and supportive with the slow meaning-
focused development of a child's oral language. Yet, we tend to expect
that in one semester of one school year the child should quickly master written language. Literacy—the act of reading and writing—is language. Therefore, literacy instruction needs to be framed in the same
patient and supportive conditions that we provide for the development of oral language. We need meaningful contexts. Children are
never provided with spoken language exercises just to practice making a sound or part of a word or phrase. Instead, spoken language is
always embedded in meaningful exchange. Children's attempts to
communicate through spoken language are always responded to with
care for their sense of themselves as worthy human beings. When
meaning is unclear, the adults tend to probe and to provide additional
language and support until the meaning is understood. Likewise, we
should embed any instruction in literacy in meaningful contexts, with
an attitude of support and tenacious pursuit of making sense of written language.

Children Bring a Wealth of Knowledge to School

Not only do children come to school with an established oral language
base, most of them also bring a wealth of print knowledge, with an
awareness of the print in their environment. The extent to which they

interpret the print will vary. However, they do indeed have repeated exposure to labels on food, toothpaste, soap, clothing, toys. In addition, there is constant exposure to logos through the bombardment of television advertisements. Most children will recognize the major fast food franchises and many of the other logos so prominently displayed through television. There will be exposure to stories as well. Some more than others. Some will have heard the stories of their parents, grandparents, aunts, uncles, and cousins telling of family antics, tragedies, and sharing of sweet memories. Many will have been read to frequently. Others will have been read to only sporadically. And some will have very little history of sitting with a significant adult snuggled and safe, bathed in the soothing voice of security. All children will have some experience with print and some notions about what readers and writers do and how they go about it. It is our job to zero in on that experience and continue building, broadening the base and spiraling upward connecting story to story, life to story, language to story.

Instruction Needs to Be Provided in a Supportive Environment

One thing I have learned in my own teaching life is that students thrive more under supportive conditions than under punitive ones. In general, we tend to avoid those tasks, activities, and opportunities in life where we believe we will not be successful. We tend to avoid the possibility of being punished or humiliated. For teaching/learning to be effective and efficient then, it makes sense that we focus our efforts in those areas around positive, supportive, and success-building environments.

Reading Materials Should Be Authentic

Inasmuch as literacy is language and language is social and meaningful, we must provide our students with reading material that consists of real language. The materials we use for supporting children as readers must be written by people with something to say. That is, what we give children to read should be written for readers, not students. I tend to avoid books, stories, etc. that are written for the purpose of teaching someone to read. Instead, I select materials that have elements I admire and that I believe will appeal to the audience I am working with. For example, I look for something where the language makes sense even without the pictures. Art should illuminate, extend, and enhance the story. Art should not be the story with words as decorations on each page. For example, a book with beautiful art depicting children running a race with words reading, "See Tom run. Tom runs fast. See Ron run. Ron runs fast. See Dan run. Dan runs fast. Run Tom. Run Ron. Run Dan. Run, run, run." Clearly, the point of such a "book" is to give the child practice with word identification of a few basic words. The words are for practice. The art tends to tell the story. Authentic materials are those that are written by authors for young readers. Books like *Rosie's Walk* by Pat Hutchins have very few words.

The words however, are closely wedded to Hutchins's art. The language will stand alone telling the basic story. However, the art illuminates, extends, and enhances the story.

Together, there is a richer understanding, a deeper connection for the young reader. It is clear the book was written to entertain the child and not for an adult to make instruction from.

Reading Is Understanding

Reading that does not result in the construction of meaning, that does not lead to understanding, is little more than word identification. That is, the "reader" has done little more than identify a list of words strung together in sentences and paragraphs. We must be cautious that neither reading instruction nor reading materials leave children with the impression that reading is primarily an act of getting the words right. Rather, children who will be successful readers—independent readers—are those who constantly question the writer and ask themselves, "Does that make sense?" Clearly, we want our children to have the necessary strategies and skills for identifying words. However, the single, focused outcome in the act of reading is to make sense of the written language. What has the reader gained if he or she has correctly pronounced all the words without understanding what has been read? Would the reader be better served to have misread *house* as *home* and *street* as *road* and to have understood the meaning? The point is that any "reading" of text that does not result in meaning making or understanding is less than efficient, even if all the words were pronounced correctly.

Meaning and Making Sense Must Serve as the Frame for Considering Skills

Since reading is understanding, one must assume that the ultimate goal of reading instruction is to arrive at the construction of meaning, to make sense, to understand. Therefore, any emphasis given to the development of skills would be done so within the frame of how the skill being emphasized would assist the reading toward the goal of reading for meaning.

Example Situations

Consider the following situations. Each of these scenarios is organized to give you a thumbnail sketch of some of the possibilities. As you read you will find a situation introducing a child and a bit of literacy history. This will be followed by some things for you to consider before taking action and a few suggestions for working with the specific situation. This in turn is followed by a brief description of how the principles above are working in each situation. As you read, pause after each situation and note what you would do if you found yourself working with the child featured. Then compare your initial reactions to the considerations and suggestions given. Where there are differences in what is presented here and in your initial reactions you might want to talk the situation through with your host teacher or the coordinator of your volunteer project. Clearly what is presented here is by no means an exhaustive list of possibilities. Many things must be considered, and each situation involves an individual child with his or her personal history. These situations are here merely to acquaint you with some of the possibilities and to provide a demonstration of the thinking process you might adopt before taking action when working with children in literacy development.

SITUATION: NATHAN, AGE 7, GRADE 2

Nathan brings a copy of *Frog and Toad Together* to his third meeting with you. As you listen to him read you notice that when he comes to an unfamiliar word he almost always stops and looks up at you. Occasionally, he will attempt to sound out the first letter, but usually he just sits looking at you and waiting.

HAVE YOU THOUGHT ABOUT . . .

◆ whether Nathan has had adequate time to become familiar and comfortable with you? Could he be searching for cues from you as to how you wish to deal with unfamiliar words? Remember that adults don't all agree on what is best for children in many situations. Nathan has lived long enough to discover that different adults have different expectations. He may be simply feeling his way through to find your expectations.

◆ what Nathan typically does when confronted with an unfamiliar word while reading in the classroom alone or in a small group?

◆ whether Nathan believes that the good readers are those who get all the words right?

◆ whether Nathan believes that he will be corrected or criticized for missing a word?

HAVE YOU TRIED . . .

◆ asking Nathan what he usually does when he is reading alone and comes to an unfamiliar word?

◆ encouraging him to skip over the word and read on to the end of the sentence, paragraph, or page when he comes to a word that causes him to stop and look at you?

◆ asking him to read through a section of the story or text, then stopping to retell that section? Does he understand what he has read? Is the individual word critical to the meaning of the story? Can he return to the word with the meaning of the whole and make sense of the word he had trouble with?

◆ showing Nathan how to preview the material before reading. On a sticky note make a list of any of the words you expect him to stop on. Then you could try any of the following:

✔ Cover those words with a small sticky note and read along with Nathan. Tell Nathan that when he comes to one of those places, he can just keep going. At the end of the selection have him retell the story. Ask yourself: Does Nathan understand what he has read? Is the individual word critical to the meaning of the story? Can he return to the covered words with the meaning of the whole and make sense of them?

✔ Cover those words with a small sticky note and have Nathan listen and follow along. While you are reading aloud for Nathan, model the above strategy for him to see how readers make sense of unfamiliar text. As you complete the selection, retell what you read. Go back into the text and stop at each covered word and use the context to show what the word might be. Uncover the word and use the letters/sounds to verify your attempts. By thinking aloud at these points in the text you can show Nathan how readers use the cues of language to identify unknown words. As you verify those words that had been covered, continue reading softly—just say the word and allow him to join in again when and where he is comfortable with the text.

Literacy Develops over Time

Remember that you are working with Nathan because he needs more time, more attention, more demonstrations, and guidance. Not only does he need time on the clock and the calendar, but he also needs time with books, time listening to language in story and text, time in the presence of a literacy mentor who will live out the strategies he is trying to develop.

Reading Is Understanding

Remember that getting the words right is only one concrete way the world has to determine whether a person did read. However, when getting the words right becomes a child's (or adult's) definition of reading, the focus is shifted away from making sense and constructing meaning—understanding. Continuously demonstrate through your comments, questions, strategies, and other interactions with Nathan that the goal of reading is to make sense of what is written.

Instruction Needs to Be Provided in a Supportive Environment

Remember that you cannot teach Nathan if you cannot reach Nathan. In other words, he has to understand that you are there to support him and guide him. He has to know, without doubt, that he can trust you to honor and respect his honest attempts. No child (indeed no student of any age) will take the risk to explore with new strategies and ideas unless the teacher, tutor, mentor has demonstrated his or her trustworthiness. From the first moment you meet you must always focus your demonstrations and instruction in ways that support Nathan's strengths and lead him to grow into the next possibility.

SITUATION: MEG, AGE 9, GRADE 3

In your meetings with Meg you notice that she gets most words right as she reads aloud for you. When there is a word she falters on, she usually stops and quietly sounds the word out. She doesn't always come up with the correct pronunciation, but she seems confident that she is correct. At times she comes up with a pronunciation that does not even sound like a word, but she continues to move along in the text. When she reaches the end of the story or selection she remembers only a few facts and details. She has difficulty summarizing or retelling the story. She also has a difficult time making connections between events in the story.

HAVE YOU THOUGHT ABOUT . . .

◆ whether this pattern is typical when Meg reads aloud?

◆ whether Meg shows any sign of looking for meaning while reading? Does she make comments like, "Oh, I didn't think he would do that next." Or "Mmmm, that doesn't make sense."

◆ whether she ever rereads a line, sentence, or paragraph to gain context for those unfamiliar words?

◆ whether she ever reads on beyond the unfamiliar word to gain context?

◆ whether, when Meg reads in her class, the students are encouraged to discuss the story, sharing their connections, interpretations, insights, and confusions?

◆ the books Meg usually reads from in class? Read through a few of the selections yourself. Is there a significant story line? Are the characters believable, do they have personality? Is there conflict or tension in the plot that gives the characters something to do? In short, is there a story? Is there real language? Or does it seem that the purpose of the material is more one of providing practice with identifying words?

HAVE YOU TRIED . . .

◆ reading a short story, a picture book, or a traditional tale to Meg, having her listen to the story without the task of decoding the print? Try it. After reading aloud for her, ask Meg to retell the story to you. This will help you determine whether Meg can focus on the overall frame of the story. If you find that Meg is able to retell the story that you read aloud to her, you can be fairly comfortable with the notion that she can also manage the same when reading similar material on her own.

◆ selecting meaningful reading material with Meg and having her read the piece in chunks? You could preread the text and place a self-stick note on the page at the most critical junctures. I'd select those places where the characters have a dilemma or conflict that must be resolved and the author has not yet revealed the solution. Meg's focus would be on naming the issue, conflict, dilemma and making some prediction about how the character(s) might resolve it. She could just jot down her thoughts on the self-stick note and move it as she reads on to determine the outcome. In most stories or chapters there would be only two to four places where you would logically stop for this sort of thinking. You might find it necessary to read the selections together so that Meg learns how to identify those critical junctures in the plot. That is essential to having her able to use the strategy in your absence. And remember, our goal is to develop readers and writers who function independently. Therefore, we should focus on strategies that are both lasting and transportable. That is, we need to give our students those strategies that will work in many situations and ones that can be used without us present to validate them.

Reading Is Understanding

Here again, a key point is to help developing readers of any age broaden their definitions of reading. Meg's actions provide windows to her beliefs about reading. Her use of "sounding it out" to arrive at a nonword and then continuing on to the end could signal that in her thoughts a good reader is one who can pronounce all the words and "read" to the end. The difficulty she has with summarizing or retelling is a signal that she doesn't see reading as a meaning-making process. This leads us right into another key principle.

Meaning and Making Sense Must Serve as the Frame for Considering Skills

Reading strategies and habits are acquired through consistent demonstration. Meg has most likely been told over and over to "sound it out." She may have even been interrupted during her reading to be told that she had gotten a word wrong. The implicit message she has heard over and over is that good readers use these skills and always get the words right. In situations like these it is very easy for the child to gradually shift attention away from understanding the language to pronouncing all the words. We must remember that any skill can be overemphasized, that no skill is the panacea, that unless the reader constructs meaning from the reading, the skill has proven fruitless. Clearly, there are many useful, essential skills and strategies that readers need to develop. Let us remember the function of each of them is to assist the reader in making sense of the print.

Reading Materials Should Be Authentic

Remember that Meg can read for meaning only if there is sense and meaning in the material she is reading. Many of the materials developed for reading instruction focus more heavily on decodable print and patterns in language than on telling a story. If Meg is to use her reading skills and strategies to make sense of the story, to get at the meaning, there must be identifiable characters with some depth and personality. The story must be couched in a setting that can be imagined, that is clearly establishing a sense of place for the characters to act. The actions of the characters must be played out in a plot that allows the characters to deal with issues, conflict, tension, resolutions, etc. In essence, there must be a story and not just a collection of words strung together just to give the child practice in applying the skill of the week (*The fat cat sat on a mat. The thin pin is in the fat mat. The fat pig can do a jig*).

SITUATION: ERICA, AGE 6, GRADE 1

While working with Erica you notice that she seems to be "frozen to the page" each time you listen to her read. It seems that she struggles with words and seems to move through even simple text at a slow, tedious pace.

HAVE YOU THOUGHT ABOUT . . .

◆ how often Erica has the opportunity to hear fluent reading models in her daily routines?

◆ the words Erica seems to have control over in her reading?

◆ the typical strategies you have seen Erica employ when encountering an unfamiliar word?

◆ whether she tends to use the same strategy when reading back her own words?

◆ whether she writes her own thoughts and language?

◆ whether she recognizes words in the story as you read aloud to her

◆ whether she recognizes and identifies the logos commonly used in her community?

HAVE YOU TRIED . . .

◆ reading aloud to her at every meeting? Choose something she enjoys and read to her with smooth, fluent expression. Don't be fake and overdramatic; just be sincere and read with a voice you'd enjoy listening to. Remember, your purpose here is not to teach her new words or strategies for identifying words. Here the point is to give Erica a sampling of the beautiful language, vivid images, chilling adventures, warm memories that can lie in wait among the words and pages of books. Your job, then, is to provide consistent exposure to great stories and proficient, fluent models of reading. It is important for young readers to hear the rhythms and cadences of language read aloud. Just as in other aspects of learning, the student needs to see print, observe the strategies of a good reader in use, to hear the language of authors come to life through the voice of a proficient reader. Having this consistent demonstration provides the young reader with the experience to envision what readers do when they interact with print, to create a "sound image" of the voice of written language.

◆ providing a selection of predictable books for Erica to listen to, read alongside you, and read for you? (See appendix for a list of predictable books you might use.) If you read *Brown Bear, Brown Bear* aloud and let Erica see the illustrations and print as you read, she could both see and hear the patterns in the language and the additional support provided by the illustrations. After you have read the book to her once or twice, invite her to read along if she hasn't already done so on her own. Pause where you can allow Erica to chime in, using the clues from these patterns to

identify words in the story. As you read together note which clues and patterns Erica seems to use. Take the opportunity to point out any additional clues along the way.

◆ having Erica use taped read-alongs? She could have a selection of "comfortable" books, those books she has read successfully and has confidence and control with. Using these "comfortable" books, Erica can listen to the tape and read along. Beginning this process with "comfortable" books is important because these allow Erica to focus on rhythm, flow, and cadence in the voice of the taped reading. As she listens and silently follows along she is rehearsing that rhythm, flow, and cadence—fluency. After listening and reading along silently she will be invited to read along aloud. You could have her listen with earphones or without. Using earphones will provide a continuous model and support while you have the opportunity to hear her read along and note her progress.

Children Bring a Wealth of Knowledge to School

Erica has six years of experience in the world as a language user. She listens, initiates, and responds in conversations. She can recall events in detail and sequence from this morning and from her last birthday party—a year ago. She lives in a world virtually littered with print—billboards, street signs, advertising, labels, logos, magazines, and newspapers. She, like most children, is a frequent viewer of television. She interacts with family and friends with ease. Erica has favorite family stories, memories from birthdays and holidays, knowledge of rules for the games she plays with other kids who live near her. Through television she knows about places she has never visited. She has an extensive collection of shells and thinks of herself as an expert. Remember that knowing the child is essential to teaching the child. All that experience, all that knowledge, all that language is the foundation upon which you will build. Think of the power of books and stories you two could develop around family tales, rules for games, classifying the shell collection.

Literacy Is Language

Remember that it is language we read and write. Clearly there are differences between written and spoken language, but they are both language. Because this is so, the child's facility with spoken language should be used as a bridge to written language. Developing Erica's ear for the flow and rhythm of written language in stories gives her a way to anticipate the writer that parallels her ability to anticipate a speaker and finish his or her sentence. Developing her ear for the language of stories, poems, information books builds a frame for her to use as a writer just as the language of her most immediate family builds the frame for her first attempts with speech. Erica's reading and writing are grounded in her listening and speaking. Literacy is language.

Literacy Develops over Time

Here again, it is essential to remember that learning occurs over time through repeated demonstrations by others who play a significant role in the child's life. Erica is six years old. Continuously provide demonstrations of what you hope she will grow into. Show how you use the strategies and skills you hope she will develop for herself. Demonstrate how those important pieces help you to make sense of the written language in the world. Telling about it is never enough. You must live it out before her very eyes

and it must be tied to something she finds relevant. Once is never enough. It takes time.

Meaning and Making Sense Must Serve as the Frame for Considering Skills

Remember that skills are useful only when they lead to making sense and helping the child understand the written language. Remember that skills and strategies are useful only when they can be utilized independently by the child. That is, when the teacher/tutor/mentor is not present to verify the outcome. In Erica's case it would be too easy to jump to the conclusion that what she needs is an array of word-attack skills. Just remember that any skill, in order to be useful, must be presented in the context of its function. That is to say that Erica has to learn skills and strategies as they are useful to her in the process of making sense of print.

SITUATION: TRENT, AGE 7, GRADE 1

As you read with Trent, you notice that his confidence is much greater as a reader than as a writer. He tends to select books that are appropriate to his proficiency. When selecting books of high interest that are beyond his own ability, he seeks someone to read aloud to him. When he reads aloud, there is confidence in his voice and he uses "story inflection." Although he has good strategies for identifying unfamiliar words and good fluency when reading aloud, he frequently skips entire lines of the story.

HAVE YOU THOUGHT ABOUT . . .

◆ why Trent sometimes skips entire lines while reading aloud?

◆ why he might be so reluctant to write even though he seems to have developed some good reading strategies?

◆ Trent's ability to select materials at the appropriate level for his purposes?

◆ the possibility that Trent's reluctance to write could be linked to his ability as a reader and sense of self as a literate individual?

◆ that his reluctance to write may result from the power of his ability as a reader? For example, he may be unwilling to attempt committing his thoughts to print when he is very aware of the fact that what he writes is not like what he sees in the books he reads. Because of that awareness, Trent may be less likely to commit to writing all those words he uses in speaking and can identify when reading.

HAVE YOU TRIED . . .

◆ encouraging Trent to use a bookmark to slide down the page as he reads? The bookmark could cover the lines of print he has read. This would help focus his attention on upcoming text and help with his habit of skipping entire lines of print.

◆ using a "talking book" to encourage Trent to write? This can be a notebook dedicated to conversations you have with Trent where neither of you speak. You write to him and he responds to you, like e-mail in a notebook. The point here is twofold. One, you provide a constant demonstration of putting thoughts and ideas in print. Two, you provide an opportunity for Trent to write for a clearly identified audience that is non-judgmental. That is to say that you, as audience, will be the only one to read the conversations, you are present to clarify when necessary and do not hold the power of grading the work. The book has an added benefit, that is, it becomes a permanent record of progress.

Language Is Social

Remember that language is a means of sharing what is known. Trent clearly understands the potential of language to communicate the ideas of others, as he is developing as a proficient reader. He has a well-developed expressive vocabulary as a speaker and initiates as well as responds in conversation. Here you have the opportunity to help him realize the same potentials in written language. The language potentials he has realized as a reader can be useful in helping him to develop as a writer.

Instruction Needs to Be Provided in a Supportive Environment

Remember that Trent has many strengths as a learner and as a language user. Be careful to provide demonstrations for Trent that build on these strengths and allow him to make approximations or try out new things as a reader/writer without fear or penalty.

Children Bring a Wealth of Knowledge to School

Trent brings not only his experience in the world, he also brings successful strategies as reader. As with any child, the wise among us would make use of this knowledge as a foundation for other learning. Trent's confidence and competence as a reader can be a useful hinge for growing him into an equally confident and competent writer.

SITUATION: EDDIE, AGE 8, GRADE 2

In your very first meetings with Eddie, it becomes clear that he has very little confidence as a reader. He is reluctant to attempt print and generally responds, "I don't know that word," or "I can't read." If nudged, he will struggle with the first sound, make a random guess, pick out the few words he knows, or create a story to explain the illustrations when they are present.

HAVE YOU THOUGHT ABOUT . . .

◆ what has stripped Eddie of his confidence as a reader? Building an image of oneself as a reader is something that occurs over time. It is through several successful experiences with print that this sense of self slowly builds. Losing that confidence is also something that occurs over time. It is unlikely that a single event would be the cause. Therefore, it is worth the time to explore how Eddie has developed this image of himself.

◆ how you can help Eddie regain the confidence and reestablish that sense of self he needs to move forward? What can you do during each meeting with Eddie that will build both confidence and competence?

◆ the significant impact of self-confidence upon performance? Think about your own experiences in life. Don't you usually do better in those areas or tasks you believe you will be successful in? Don't you experience much greater anxiety over those tasks that you believe yourself less competent in? In many ways, confidence is gained through successful attempts at a task or experience. Likewise, confidence can fuel further attempts. This cycle leads to competence. In short, confidence begets competence.

◆ the knowledge of story-structure and language that Eddie must have? In order to create a story to explain the illustration, Eddie must have an understanding of the structure and organization of stories. He must also have a grasp of the language used in stories. The key here is to learn to recognize and attend to the strengths a child brings to any experience. It is much too easy to focus on the deficits, that is, what the child can't do. When it becomes our focus, we too often fail to see what the child can do.

◆ how could you build on Eddie's knowledge of story structure and language to advance his confidence and proficiency as a reader?

HAVE YOU TRIED . . .

◆ working with Eddie to create a book of labels, logos, and print from advertising and product packaging? You could bring several sales papers from the local area and ask Eddie to bring some logos and labels from products he uses at home. Ask Eddie to sort through them and select those he can read. Clip those he selects and ask him to name them for you. As he does, he could paste them in a blank book. I'd suggest one item per page. As you complete a few, review the

pages asking Eddie to read the logo on each page. As he names the product, confirm his reading; then write in clear, bold print *This is* _____. In the blank you would write the word Eddie provides. For example, if *JIF* is the logo he selects, and he reads it as *peanut butter*, you'd write *This is peanut butter.* Here you'll have a common pattern (*This is* _____) on each page. The new word on each page will be keyed to the logo featured there. Eddie's familiarity with the logo will provide the support to take the risk to believe himself able to read the page. This security will give Eddie successful experience and a context for developing skills.

◆ inviting Eddie to tell the story presented in a wordless picture book (a list is provided in the appendix). As Eddie tells the story presented in the illustrations, you can write his "text" on sticky notes to accompany each illustration or spread. Place the notes on the appropriate pages as they are written. As each page is completed, re-read it with Eddie or invite him to read it for you. When the entire story is complete read it back to Eddie as he follows along and listens for anything he might like to change. When you've read it through twice and he is satisfied with the text, you might rewrite it on sticky notes or type it on a word processor so that you could have several copies. Eddie could have one copy of just the text. Another might be cut into strips and paper clipped to the pages to approximate typical book print. Once again, you provide a support system for him. The illustrations that stimulated Eddie's language for the text will still be there. Eddie's language will be there as well on the sticky notes or from the word processor. Again, you demonstrate that ideas, images, experiences are expressed through language which can be captured in one form through print, which can be revisited again and again through reading.

◆ using a similar process, you can create several new texts for Eddie to read. Use any significant event, photo, comic strip or memory that Eddie indicates an interest in. Talk with him about the event and make notes. Use the notes together with Eddie to stimulate elaboration, adding details, sequencing, and generation of a written draft. Encourage Eddie to write as much of this as possible. Although you are generating a text for Eddie to improve his reading confidence and competence, you must also attend to the whole of his language development. That of course, includes his development as a listener, as a speaker, as a reader, and as a writer. And inasmuch as language is a dynamic thinking process, you will sharpen his ability to reason, consider multiple points of view, observe, question, categorize, classify, and articulate his insights and confusions.

Literacy Develops over Time

It is true that Eddie has had time on the clock and on the calendar; he is eight years old. But, remember that it is more than the passing of minutes, days, months, and years that developing readers need. They need to spend time engaging in purposeful and meaningful interactions with written and spoken language. Just as it takes time to develop confidence and competence, it also takes time to slowly dissolve those same attitudes and abilities. The essential piece is how the time is spent, which takes us into the next principle.

Instruction Needs to Be Provided in a Supportive Environment

Sometimes the most well-intended instruction may be perceived by the child as foreign, intrusive, abstract, and confusing. Providing instruction in a supportive environment is less about your intentions and genuine caring than it is about building on what the child knows and understands. Clearly the child needs your emotional support, that is, your kindness and empathy. More important to the child's success is the support you provide by ensuring that materials are relevant to the child's experience and interest, by ensuring that the strategies you demonstrate are clearly connected to making sense of written language, by ensuring that the strategies you demonstrate are ones the child will be able to use even when you are not there to verify, and by assuring the child that you will continue providing the demonstrations as long as they are necessary.

Reading Materials Should Be Authentic

Remember that for Eddie to construct meaning from the text using the strategies you demonstrate, there must be meaningful language on the page. To be authentic, the material has to be relevant to Eddie and in language that could stand alone outside the world of school and reading instruction. Remember, if the materials were written to provide nothing more than practice pronouncing words and practice implementing a particular rule, then there is nothing authentic about them. And in that case they will be all the more abstract and meaningless to Eddie.

CHAPTER 3

Learning from Readers

"Reading" Your Partner

As young children read aloud, you have an excellent opportunity to observe closely and listen carefully to the strategies and strengths each child brings to the text. In the following samples note the original text in standard type. The child's reading of that text will be in italics and following each sample there will be some commentary with points to consider. As you read, keep in mind that the differences between the child's reading and the text are not to be viewed as "bad" or as "errors." Rather, focus on what the child is doing well. Try to consider what the reader has done to arrive at a reading different from the text. What cues has the reader missed? What cues did the reader over-rely upon? As you consider the following, think through the commentary and consider all the insight you can gain from observing readers carefully. You should also keep in mind that this is an unrehearsed reading. Each of these children was seeing these books for the first time in this classroom.

◄ **IN THIS SECTION**

Sample Scenarios for Miscue Assessment

- *Willow, Age 7, Grade 2*
- *Dakota, Age 7, Grade 2*
- *Sonia, Age 7, Grade 2*
- *Marcus, Age 7, Grade 2*

Hattie was a big black hen. One morning she looked up and said, "Goodness gracious me! I can see a nose in the bushes!" "Good grief!" said the goose.

"Good. Good grate!" said the goose.

"Good grief!" said the goose.
"Good grief!" said the duck.

≺ Note that in a previous line Hattie had said, "Goodness gracious." Perhaps this led Willow to expect the next character to repeat the expression. She may have predicted the expression and then recognized the difference. It is not uncommon for our minds to anticipate the text. As her eyes caught up with her voice she may have noticed the difference in the two expressions. It is also interesting to note the similarities between *grief* and *grate*. One concern here is that Willow did not see the lack of meaning in the expression "Good grate."

Then, a few pages later . . .

≺ Note here that Willow now recognizes the word *grief* although she misreads it earlier and now shifts from *goose* to *duck*. This substitution continues from this point on. Clearly, the two words look nothing alike. The initial sounds are made in different parts of the mouth. This is not a problem with Willow's ability to use phonics or with her ability to use other word-identification skills. Instead, it would appear that she has become rather comfortable with the sequence in which each of the animals will speak (Hattie, goose,

"Good grief!" said the goose.

"Goodness grief!" said the duck.

"I can see a nose, two eyes, two ears, two legs, and a body in the bushes."

"I can see a nose, two eyes, two ears, two legs, and a sack in the bushes."

pig, sheep, horse, cow). In addition, she is also referring to the illustrations, and many children, being more familiar with ducks than with geese, would refer to the illustration of a goose as a duck. It would seem that young Willow is doing what many adults would do if reading this story aloud for an audience. That is, she seems to trust her memory on those lines that are repeated in each scene.

A few pages later, Willow continues with . . .

≺ Note that here there seems to be more evidence that Willow is trusting her memory and only using the print to validate her expectation. *Goodness* for *Good* is clearly carried forward from Hattie's expression and attributed to the goose/duck. This is not repeated with the expressions of the other characters.

Later, she continues . . .

≺ Note here that in each scene leading up to this one there has been a cumulative pattern of revealing yet another body part. In each scene all the previous parts are mentioned again, and the new one is added at the end. A young reader might not expect the torso or *body* to be one of the body parts. Clearly the text says *body.* Again, however, as readers we all rely on a number of cues as we make sense of text. What this does reveal is that Willow is attending to the author's use of patterns, the repeating of things, and the adding of a new detail. It also reveals that Willow is attending to the significant role of illustrations in a picture book. The revelation of a sack is sensible in this plot as the fox could clearly be planning to bag one of the farm animals for his meal. As Willow follows the building suspense in which parts of the fox are revealed, it is also clear to her that there is impending danger. Her knowledge of the role a fox character usually plays in stories would lead her to anticipate such action as bagging his lunch. A sack would be a logical item to reveal next.

Then a few lines later . . .

"I can see a nose, two eyes, two ears, a body, four legs, and a tail in the bushes!"

"I can see a nose, two eyes, two ears, two back, four legs and a tail in the bushes!"

≺ Note here that the expectation of a sack did not pan out. Instead, Hattie reveals even more body parts. Perhaps Willow does not find it sensible that the body parts would be named separately with the torso (body) included among them, and her need for meaning moves her onward. Here again we would need to ask Willow what she was thinking as she read this segment of the text.

But the cow said, "MOO!"
so loudly that the fox was
frightened and ran away.

**But the cow said, "MOO!"
so——"MOO!" so——[long
pause and teacher supplies the
word]—loudly that the fox was
frightened and ran away.**

And they were all so surprised
that none of them said
anything for a very long time.

Willow continues with the text, and then a few lines later . . .

≺ Note that this is the only place in the story where Willow pauses
long enough that the teacher feels it necessary to supply the unfamiliar word. Willow does demonstrate the strategy of rereading to
gain context. In this case though, it does not seem to help. She
does not read the text following the unfamiliar word, at least she
does not read it aloud. Perhaps she reads it silently during the long
pause and does not find that it provides any clue to the word
loudly. When the teacher does supply the word, Willow is able to
move on and to complete the text.

Stop That Rabbit ◆ by Sharon Peters

Mrs. Baker had a garden.

Mr. *[long pause with no attempt, and teacher supplies the word]* **Baker had a g—** *[attempts the first sound then moves on]* **garden.**

She had a beautiful rose garden.

She had a p— *[attempts first sound as "p" then recognizes his error]* **beautiful rose garden.**

The roses had long stems and big leaves.

The roses had long st— st— stems and big leaves.

≺ Note that in each case here, Dakota relies upon attempting the initial sound of an unfamiliar word as his first strategy. This is a pattern that you will see throughout the remainder of the story. The reading of *Mrs.* as *Mr.* could be his expectation for the character to be male or a limited knowledge with abbreviations. He does seem to attend to meaning as he continues.

Jane lived next door.

Jan lived next door.

Jane loved roses.

Jan loved roses.

Jane loved to smell the roses.

Jan lived loved to smell the roses.

She loved to touch the roses. But Jane never picked the roses.

But Jan n— n— never picked the roses.

≺ You will note that Dakota's reading of *Jane* as *Jan* will be consistent throughout the story. Perhaps he saw the first letters and ignored the "e," perhaps he does not recognize the influence of "e" in words such as *lake, like, smile, Jane.* Because of his attention to initial sounds, it would seem logical that he recognizes *Jan* as a name and tends to ignore the "e." In any case, he is consistent. That in itself is noteworthy.

≺ Note that Dakota tends to self-correct as he reads. Whenever his reading differs from the text he almost always self-corrects. It seems that he is very conscious of getting words right. In this situation *lived* or *loved* would make sense in the sentence. In fact, either word would essentially maintain the same meaning. Therefore, there is little indication that it was meaning that signaled Dakota to return and correct the word.

≺ Note that Dakota tends to repeat the initial sound of unfamiliar words. One recurring strategy for him is to "sound it out." In this reading it appears, however, that he limits his attempts with this strategy only to the initial sound.

Mrs. Baker watered the roses.

Miss Baker watered the roses.

One day, Mrs. Baker was very mad.

One day, Miss Baker was very mad.

Someone picked the roses. The roses were bent and broken.

The roses were b— b— b— [short pause] broke . . . be gone . . . [long pause with no attempt to move on and teacher supplies the word] bent and broken.

≺ Note here that Dakota has picked up on the pronoun *she* and now reads *Mrs.* as *Miss.* The teacher notes this as reading that differs from the text; however, it could be a part of Dakota's speech pattern to use the two (*Mrs., Miss*) interchangeably. Perhaps this is something the teacher has been working on and feels the children should recognize. In either case, you will note that from this point on Dakota continues with this substitution. Clearly he recognizes that the character is female now.

≺ Again Dakota's attempt with "sounding it out" is limited to the initial consonant. Note the hesitation that follows when he is confronted with unfamiliar text and his primary strategy fails him. He seems to attempt to insert a word that would make sense and would begin with the same initial consonant. Although this is a useful strategy for independent reading, Dakota lacks sufficient confidence to continue and just waits for his teacher to supply the word.

"Who picked the roses?" said
Mrs. Baker

"Who picked the roses?" said
Miss Baker.

"Jane, Did you pick the roses?"

"Jan, Did you pick the roses?"

"No," said Jane.

"No, the" [inserts the, pauses
and rereads] *"No," said Jan.*

"I never pick the roses."
"The roses are bent and
broken," said Mrs. Baker.

"The roses are bent and
broken," said Miss Baker.

Mrs. Baker sat and waited.

Ms. Baker sat down and [long
pause, teacher supplies the word
and the child returns to sat and
repeats] *sat and waited.*

≺ Here Dakota seems to anticipate the text to continue a conversation about the roses. As he reads on and recognizes the word *said*, his miscue becomes apparent and he returns to the beginning to reread.

≺ Once again Dakota appears to lack confidence in his ability to read on to make sense of the text. Note that he makes a sensible insertion *sat down* which would likely be used in his own speech. However, when the text fails to meet his expectation he seems thrown by words he has demonstrated control over in many other settings. He simply pauses and waits for the teacher to come to his rescue.

And Jane sat and waited.

And Jan sat and waited.

"Stop!" said Jane.

"Stop!" said Jan.

"Stop that rabbit!"

"Stop that rabbit! Stop that rabbit!"

"The rabbit is in the rose garden!"

"The rabbit is in the rose garden! The rabbit is in the rose garden!"

"The rabbit is hungry," said Mrs. Baker.

"The rabbit is happy [pause] hungry," said Miss Baker.

≺ Here it seems that Dakota is taken with the excitement in this phrase and repeats the line as we might expect any character to do in this situation. This demonstrates that Dakota is thinking about the story and is anticipating the text, just as we have seen in some of his previous miscues.

≺ It is interesting to note that once again he tends to self-correct as he reads. Just as in the segment above when he first substituted *lived* for *loved* and then returned to correct, here both *happy* and *hungry* would make sense. Perhaps Dakota is anticipating the text again. All good readers do. He expects the rabbit to be happy since it has had such a lovely snack. There was no loss of meaning by this substitution. So again in this situation, there is little indication that it was meaning that signaled him to return and correct the word. Perhaps it is his concern with getting all the words "right."

The rabbit loves the long stems and leaves.

The rabbit lives. . . . The rabbit loves the long stem . . . stems and leaves.

"That is why he picked the roses," said Mrs. Baker.

"That is. . . . That is . . . [long pause with no attempt, teacher supplies the word] That is why he pulled the roses," said Miss Baker.

So Mrs. Baker and Jane fed the rabbit.

So Miss Baker had Jan . . . Baker and Jan found the rabbit.

Every day they fed the rabbit. And the rabbit never picked the roses again.

And they rabbit . . . the rabbit never picked the roses again.

≺ Here again Dakota shows little confidence using cues other than his sight-recognition of the word and attempting the initial consonant. He seems to consistently pause for the teacher to supply words when he doesn't recognize them.

EXAMPLE SCENARIO: SONIA, AGE 7, GRADE 2

A Chair for My Mother ◆ by Vera B. Williams

My mother works as a waitress in the Blue Tile Diner.

My mother works as a waitress in the Blue Tile Dinner.

After school sometimes I go to meet her there.
Then her boss Josephine gives me a job too.
I wash the salts and peppers and fill the ketchups.

I wish the salts and peppers . . . wash the salts and peppers and fill the ketchups.

≺ Sonia substitutes the word *dinner* for *diner*. First note the close similarity between the spellings of the two words. Also note that the meaning is not changed dramatically especially if we assume that Sonia has had no real-life experience with a diner.

≺ The substitution of *wish* for *wash* is immediately recognized as Sonia reads enough of the text to signal a lack of sense in the phrase. Clearly, Sonia is attending to letter-sound cues, grammar cues, and meaning cues. Her substitution is "off" by only one vowel sound—it maintains the same part of speech in the sentence,

One time I peeled all the onions for the onion soup.

One time I peeled all the onions for the onion shop.

but it fails to make sense. That is her signal to take a closer look. We want to encourage this behavior because it is an efficient strategy that will serve her well as she reads independently. This self-monitoring behavior is one of the goals we hope to help all children attain.

≺ Here again, Sonia makes a substitution that demonstrates she is indeed using all the cueing systems. Her substitution of *shop* for *soup* is understandable because the words are similar in appearance and share the same initial and final consonants; the substitution also serves the same part of speech and makes sense. Clearly, it alters the meaning of the text, but it does make sense and would not necessarily alert Sonia to her miscue.

When I finish, Josephine says, "Good work, honey," she pays me.

When I finish, Josephine says, "Good work, honey," and plays me . . . pays me.

And every time, I put half of my money into the jar.
It takes a long time to fill a jar this big.
Every day when my mother comes home from work, I take down the jar.
My mama empties all her change from tips out of her purse for me to count.
Then we push all of the coins into the jar.
Sometimes my mama is laughing when she comes home from work.
Sometimes she's so tired she falls asleep while I count the money into piles.
Some days she has lots of tips.
Some days she has only a little.
Then she looks worried.
But each evening every single shiny coin goes into the jar.

But each every day single shiny coin going . . . . goes into the jar.

≺ Just as in the substitution of *dinner* for *diner,* here the substitution of *pays* for *plays* utilizes all the cueing systems. Here again, though, it is the loss of meaning that signals Sonia to return and take a closer look. As with the earlier substitution, Sonia clearly recognizes both words. Her miscue was not because of a lack of skill with word recognition.

≺ Note that Sonia seems to expect the text to follow a common expression "each and every day." Her substitution of *every day* for *evening every* would make sense at the point of the substitution. The text that follows should signal that she needs to return and take a closer look. However, she continues on to complete the sentence.

We sit in the kitchen to count the tips.
Usually Grandma sits with us too.
While we count, she likes to hum.
Often she has money in her old leather wallet for us.

After she has money in her old letter wallet for us.

Whenever she gets a good bargain on tomatoes or bananas or

Whenever she gets a good *[long pause and teacher supplies the word]* **bargain on** *[another long pause, again the teacher supplies the word]* **tomatoes or bananas or something**

something she buys, she puts by the savings and they go into the jar.

≺ Here her substitutions of *after* for *often* and *letter* for *leather* make use of all the cueing systems. In both cases the substitution does make sense and does not significantly alter the meaning. Therefore, Sonia would have no signal that she should take a closer look. This is, of course, what proficient readers do. Even adults like you will misread a cue and substitute one word for another without realizing it unless it fails to make sense. The only time these miscues are noticeable is when you read aloud for others who have copies of the text you are reading.

≺ Note the two words Sonia finds troubling are *bargain* and *tomatoes*. Perhaps the shift in context from the mother—her work at the diner and saving her tips—to the grandmother, her old wallet,

When we can't get a single other coin into the jar, we are going to take out all the money and go and buy a chair.
Yes, a chair.
A wonderful, beautiful, fat, soft armchair.
We will get one covered in velvet with roses all over it.

We will get one covered in velvet with rose all over it.

We are going to get the best chair in the whole world.
That is because our old chairs burned up.
There was a big fire in our other house.
All our chairs burned.
So did our sofa and so did everything else.
That wasn't such a long time ago.
My mother and I were coming home from buying new shoes.
I had new sandals.
She had new pumps.

She had new plumps [no recognition of the impact on meaning and the teacher supplies the word]

shopping and finding bargains confuses her. Perhaps the words are unfamiliar and the context provides no clue to identification. It is interesting to note that Sonia doesn't tend to attempt a word unless the meaning is clear. She does show attention to the use of other cueing systems, but also seems to recognize the need for using them in combination toward the goal of making sense.

≺ Note how Sonia's substitution closely matches sound and grammar. Her use of *plumps* for *pumps* may indicate a lack of experience with the word *pumps* as a type of shoe. Perhaps *plump* is more a description of what she sees in the illustration. Perhaps it makes more sense to describe a shoe as *plump* than as a *pump*. Here again, it would be best to talk

We were walking to our house from the bus.
We were looking at everyone's tulips.
We were looking at everyone's tullops . . . tulips.

with Sonia to find out what she was thinking. Usually, there is some logical reasoning if you talk with the reader. Try to suspend your adult logic and get the child's insights. You'll generally gain some valuable information.

≺ Again, Sonia demonstrates her use of all the cueing systems. However, as is the case in most of her miscues she tends to be guided most by the need to make sense. This is clearly the mark of an independent reader. The key thing to remember is that every strategy we give to children should be something they can use when we aren't there to validate. Children have to learn to monitor their own reading, to construct meaning and make sense of print as an independent process. Clearly we must guide

She was saying she liked red tulips and I was saying I liked yellow ones.
Then we came to our block.
Right outside our house stood two big fire engines.
I could see lots of smoke.
Tall orange flames came out of the roof.
All the neighbors stood in a bunch across the street.
Mama grabbed my hand and we ran.

Mama grabbed my hand we ran . . . and we ran.

My uncle Sandy saw us and ran to us.

My uncle stood saw us and ran to us [*no recognition of the impact on meaning and the teacher calls attention to the uncle's name and supplies the word*]

Mama yelled, "Where's Mother?"
I yelled, "Where's my grandma?"
My aunt Ida waved and shouted, "She's here, she's here.

My aunt Id waved and showed, "She's here, she's here.

them and demonstrate for them, but the goal is always to lead them to independence.

≺ Although the substitution of *stood* for Sandy is one that clearly alters the meaning of the individual word, it is not one that significantly alters the meaning of the text. The act of standing would be typical as someone approaches.

She's O.K.
Don't worry."
Grandma was all right.
Our cat was safe too, though it took a while to find her.

Our cat was safe too, thought it took a while to find her.

But everything else in our whole house was spoiled.

But everything else in our world house . . . whole house was [long pause with no attempt and teacher supplies the word].

≺ The substitution of *thought* for *though* is one that does make sense here and would not likely signal Sonia that a closer look would be in order.

≺ The substitution of *world* for *whole* is one that the upcoming text signaled as a miscue that altered meaning and failed to make sense. Clearly the word *world* would be a logical possibility given the context. Again, Sonia appears to be using cueing systems in combination to find meaning. When faced with *spoiled* Sonia pauses for a long time. In earlier situations she uses letter-sound, grammar, and meaning to identify unfamiliar words. Here, the word is at the end of the sentence and there is no context to follow. Perhaps the context preceding the word is not strong

What was left of the house was turned to charcoal and ashes.
We went to stay with my mother's sister Aunt Ida and
Uncle Sandy.
Then we were able to move into the apartment downstairs.
We painted the walls yellow.
The floors were all shiny.
But the rooms were very empty.

But the rooms vere very [long pause with no attempt and teacher supplies the word] **empty.**

The first day we moved in, the neighbors brought pizza and cake and ice cream.

**The first day we moved in, the neighbors bret pizza . . .
brought pizza and cake and ice cream.**

And they brought a lot of other things too.
The family across the street brought a table and three kitchen chairs.
The very old man next door gave us a bed from when his children were little.

The very old man next door gave us a bed from when his child was little.

enough to assist her. Perhaps she is unwilling to rely upon "sounding it out" without the aid of other cues to confirm. Perhaps logic would indicate the meaning of the unfamiliar word, but she recognizes that it must begin with *sp* and does not have a word in her vocabulary to fit. It is worth noting that in most other situations she has made sensible substitutions with very similar sound features that tend to fill the same part of speech. Here she appears to be stumped, and her teacher supplies the word.

≺ Here Sonia's departure from the text maintains the general meaning. There is nothing to signal her to reread. It is interesting to note that she alters the verb to correspond with her miscue on *children*.

My other grandpa brought us his beautiful rug.

My other grandpa brought us his beautiful ring.

My mother's other sister, Sally, had made us red and white curtains.

My mother's other sister, [long pause with no attempt and the teacher supplies the name] Sally, had made us red and white shutters . . .curtains.

Mama's boss, Josephine, brought us pots and pans, silverware and dishes.
My cousin brought me her own stuffed bear.
Everyone clapped when my grandma made a speech.

Everyone clapped when my grandma made a spich . . . speech.

"You all are the kindest people," she said, "and we thank you very, very much.

"You all are the kid people . . . kindest people," she said, "and we took you . . . thank you very, very much.

It's lucky we're young and can start all over."
That was last year, but we still have no sofa and no big chairs.

That was last year, but we still have on sofa and on big chairs. . . . no sofa and no big chairs.

≺ Here again Sonia's substitution of *ring* for *rug*, though a departure from the meaning of the text, is not one that would signal her to reread.

When Mama comes home, her feet hurt.

"There's no good place for me to take the load off my feet," she says.

When Grandma wants to sit back and hum and cut up potatoes she has to get as comfortable as she can on a hard kitchen chair.

So that is how come Mama brought home the biggest jar she could find at the diner and all the coins started to go into the jar.

≺ Note that in each situation above where Sonia's reading differs from the text, she consistently recognizes the impact on meaning and rereads so that her reading matches the text.

Whistle for Willie ◆ by Ezra Jack Keats

Oh, how Peter wished he could whistle!

Oh, how Peter would he called whistle!

He saw a boy playing with his dog.
Whenever the boy whistled, the dog ran straight to him.

the boy would whistle, the dog ran to him.

≺ Marcus seems to rely on initial sounds as his primary cue to the word. You will notice that most of his substitutions do have that in common with the word in the text. However, he seems to be unaffected by the impact of his substitutions on the meaning.

≺ Here Marcus seems to omit those words he finds too unfamiliar and reads only those he recognizes.

Quick as a wink, he hid in an empty carton lying on the sidewalk.

Quicking as a walk, he had in an** [long pause with no attempt and teacher supplied the word] **empty car . . car . .carton along the walk.

Peter got out of the carton and started home.

Peter got out of the carton and sounded home.

He blew till his cheeks were tired.

He blew till his teeths . . . gums . . . cheeks were

Then, later in the story as Marcus continues reading . . .

≺ Here Marcus seems to continue his strategy of relying on the initial sound to generate a substitution. It does not seem that he is attempting to "sound out" words here as he did in an earlier passage where he substituted the word *finer* for *faster*. Note that he does have a sight vocabulary (a core of words that he recognizes on sight).

As Marcus continues later in the story . . .

≺ Note that Marcus is consistent with his strategy. It can be assumed that he has arrived at some sense of himself as a reader and has generated a notion of what readers do. A part of your task here would be to continue gathering information to build on his strategies and expand his definition of reading. Demonstrate other strategies as described earlier (see pages 41–57).

Later in the story as Marcus continues . . .

≺ It is significant to note that although the text seems difficult for him, Marcus does not give up. He continues selecting chunks of the text he can handle and does tend to focus on the key pieces of meaning.

But nothing happened.

But *[long pause with no attempt and teacher supplies the word]* **nothing . . . But nothing happened.**

He whistled all the way there, and he whistled all the way home.

He whistled along and they . . . the way there, and they . . . he whistled all the way home.

Then, as Marcus completes the story . . .

≺ Again, Marcus tends to omit words and zero in on those most crucial to making some sense of the print. Clearly, his substitutions often alter the meaning. However, the essence of the story is captured in his reading of the text.

Lessons from the Children

Let's take a moment to reflect on what these four children have helped us to understand. In the space provided take a moment to write your insights, questions, confusions. Talk with your host teacher, project coordinator, or a reading specialist in the local school about your observations and wonderings.

-

-

-

-

-

Things to Consider

Here are some things to consider. When your partner reads aloud listen carefully, make note of insights or questions. Resist the urge to interrupt and correct the child when a miscue occurs. Try to let the child recognize the loss of meaning. That's the only way the reader will ever gain the independence you are there to foster. Remember that all of the strategies you demonstrate and help your partner gain control of will only be beneficial when the child is able to use them in your absence.

These four children help us to see that when readers are guided by the need to make sense, they use an array of strategies toward that goal. Readers attend to the context and the meaning cues the context provides. Readers attend to the language and the cues provided by the structure of language, the order they understand as language users. Readers attend to the graphic and phonemic cues provided in written language, the letter-sound connections. Readers are constantly using all these cues in concert to construct meaning from written language. If, for whatever reason, a reader is depending upon one strategy without attending to meaning, you should work to broaden the child's repertoire of strategies and help the child to understand that readers are in continuous search of meaning.

These four children (Willow, Dakota, Sonia, and Marcus) help us to see that reading is far more than "sounding it out" or just getting the words right. They help remind us that limiting a reader to any single strategy is not likely to be very efficient. They help remind us that growing as a reader requires time spent with engaging stories and consistent and supportive adults who demonstrate various strategies. They help us to realize that strategies must be portable; that is, for strategies to be effective they must be ones that can be used when the mentor is not present. In addition to these insights we should note the range of strategies used by these four children. We should note that all four are in grade 2 and are seven years old. The differences in their individual abilities to manage printed language should not surprise us. We certainly would not expect the four of them to be the same height, weigh the same, know the same family stories, share an identical family structure. We wouldn't even expect them to have identical proficiency with oral language because we recognize the vast influence of all the differences in their lives. It seems rather ludicrous then, for us to set an arbitrary standard and expect the four of them to arrive there at the same moment in time.

Probably the most significant insight we can gain from these four young children is this recognition of their individuality. Meet the person, not the profile. Get to know the child, not the evaluation. Work with the human being, not the client. Share great stories with interesting and beautiful language, not the instructional material. Treat your partner as an individual, a human being with dignity and integrity. Don't reduce a child to a statistic.

Remember that young readers, especially those who are struggling, are still groping about, searching for an identity as readers and writers—to view themselves as literate beings. To a great extent, that self-image, that sense of self is defined through your interactions with the child and your reactions to the child's efforts.

It may take all your strength, all the powers of your concentration, but resist the urge to notice and point out errors, mistakes, FLAWS. I know that many of us have years of school experience, perhaps home experience, that would have us believe that good teaching includes identifying and naming the flaws of learners. In fact, our experience may have us assume that learning actually arises from constant criticism and feedback on what was done wrong. It seems from that point of view that learning would only occur when someone older or wiser or more experienced points out our flaws.

Try picking up that notion, turning it over in you hands and looking closely at all sides. In many ways, what is described above is less about critique and more about criticism. *Criticism* tends to focus on the negative and by nature tends to tear down confidence and self-image; therefore, criticism may well work against both teacher and student by reducing the likelihood that the student would either initiate or participate in the process again.

Critique, on the other hand, would tend to focus on the positive. From this point of view the older, wiser, more experienced would notice and name the qualities in the child's attempts. Point out the smartness in the strategies used and help the child grow through recognizing what he or she can and does do well.

Very few of us will thrive on constant criticism. Our chances are immensely improved when those we respect and hold in esteem name our strengths and gently suggest other ways we could use them to continue our growth.

What's that got to do with leading a child to living a literate life? Well think about this. We have lived longer. We know more. We have more experience. It is so easy to forget the incredible sense of frustration that comes with the belief that it all must be learned today. That the world is going on without you. That your peers are moving into realms you've yet to explore. That kind of fear, that frustration, that incredible sense of inadequacy can freeze you in your tracks. It is our responsibility as the older, wiser, more experienced to provide demonstrations, potentials, and manageable examples for our students.

Ralph Fletcher (1993) tells us that writers need mentors. That is, someone who has gone before them. Someone who can point out their strengths. Someone who is passionate about the work and the craft of writing. Someone who values creativity and encourages risk taking. Someone who tirelessly demonstrates new alternatives, the next possibility. Someone who knows both the frustrations of struggle and the overwhelming joy of getting it right.

Bike riders need mentors. Gardeners need mentors. Musicians need mentors. So do cooks, parents, skaters. . . . In all learning we look to those we believe know more than we do. We seek out the demonstrations of those we respect and admire, even when their first-hand consultation is not available. We look to the examples in their work. We study their process. We use their demonstrations to critique ourselves. We refine our processes and actions and move forward on the basis of their actions and products.

Readers need mentors. Young readers need to see the strategies used by those more experienced with print. Young readers need to hear those mentors employ those strategies. It is through these interactions and demonstrations that young readers begin to envision what they themselves can become.

One thing about mentors: They always strive to give only as much as their students can handle at one time. Their critique is gentle, supportive, focused, and tied to specific examples. Their advice is useful and supportive and moves the student forward. Mentors understand the struggle of growing and feed their students in bite-sized demonstrations that will nurture them on to the next possibility. With this in mind remember that in many many ways you can become a mentor to your reading partner. A mentor for leading a literate life. Each time you meet bring a new book that you've discovered and loved. Share the story and point out what there is to love there. Bring an old favorite and talk about the memories, the connections to your own life as a young reader. Don't be afraid to let your partner know the child you once were. Children need to know that their experiences are somewhat universal, that their fears are not unique, that the exhilaration they experience in reading a well-crafted story is shared by readers around the globe.

Because of your experience you can be the mentor a child is looking for. Because of your commitment you can take the time to demonstrate and have the patience for the child's pace. You can be the one who is remembered, the Mrs. Hand, the voice, and the passion of beautiful words spoken aloud. You can lead a child to a literate life. You can.

◆ APPENDIX ◆
Books for Children

Alphabet Books

AGARD, JOHN. 1989. *The Calypso Alphabet*. New York: Holt.

ANNO, MITSUMASA. 1975. *Anno's Alphabet: An Adventure in Imagination*. New York: HarperCollins.

AYLESWORTH, JIM. 1992. *The Folks in the Valley: A Pennsyvania Dutch ABC*. New York: HarperCollins.

BASE, GRAEME. 1987. *Animalia*. New York: H.N. Abrams.

BAYER, JANE. 1984. *A, My Name is Alice*. New York: Dial.

CARLSON, NANCY. 1997. *ABC I Like Me!* New York: Viking.

COATS, LAURA JANE. 1993. *Alphabet Garden*. New York: Macmillan Publishing Company.

DOUBILET, ANNE. 1991. *Under the Sea from A to Z*. Photographs by David Doubilet. New York: Crown.

EHLERT, LOIS. 1989. *Eating the Alphabet: Fruits and Vegetables from A to Z*. San Diego: Harcourt Brace.

FEELINGS, MURIEL. 1974. *Jambo Means Hello: Swahili Alphabet Book*. New York: Dial.

HOBAN, TANA. 1982. *A, B, See!* New York: Greenwillow.

JOHNSON, JEAN. 1988. *Sanitation Workers, A to Z*. New York: Walker.

JOHNSON, STEPHEN T. 1995. *Alphabet City*. New York: Viking.

LOBEL, ANITA. 1990. *Alison's Zinnia*. New York: Greenwillow.

LOBEL, ANITA AND ARNOLD. 1981. *On Market Street*. New York: Greenwillow.

MARTIN, BILL, JR. AND JOHN ARCHAMBAULT. 1989. *Chicka Chicka Boom Boom*. New York: Simon & Schuster.

POMEROY, DIANA. 1997. *Wildflower ABC: An Alphabet of Potato Prints.* San Diego: Harcourt Brace.

RANKIN, LAURA. 1991. *The Handmade Alphabet.* New York: Dial.

ROSENBLUM, RICHARD. 1986. *The Airplane ABC.* New York: Atheneum.

RYDEN, HOPE. 1988. *Wild Animals of America ABC.* New York: Lodestar Books.

SENDAK, MAURICE. 1962. *Alligators All Around: An Alphabet.* New York: Harper & Row.

SHANNON, GEORGE. 1996. *Tomorrow's Alphabet.* New York: Greenwillow.

VAN ALLSBURG, CHRIS. 1987. *The Z Was Zapped.* Boston: Houghton Mifflin.

Picture Books for Reading Aloud and Sharing with Your Partner

BAKER, KEITH. 1989. *The Magic Fan.* San Diego: Harcourt Brace.

_____. 1991. *Hide and Snake.* San Diego: Harcourt Brace.

_____. 1994. *Big Fat Hen.* San Diego: Harcourt Brace.

BAYLOR, BYRD. 1974. *Everybody Needs A Rock.* New York: Charles Scribner.

_____. 1986. *I'm in Charge of Celebrations.* New York: Charles Scribner.

_____. 1994. *The Table Where Rich People Sit.* New York: Maxwell Macmillan International.

CANNON, JANELL. 1993. *Stellaluna.* San Diego: Harcourt Brace.

_____. 1997. *Verdi.* San Diego: Harcourt Brace.

DAKOS, KALLI. 1990. *If You're Not Here, Please Raise Your Hand: Poems About School.* New York: Four Winds Press.

_____. 1993. *Don't Read This Book, Whatever You Do!: More Poems About School.* New York: Four Winds Press.

DEEDY, CARMEN AGRA. 1991. *Agatha's Feather Bed: Not Just Another Wild Goose Story.* Atlanta: Peachtree Publishers, Ltd.

_____. 1993. *Tree Man.* Atlanta: Peachtree Publishers, Ltd.

_____. 1994. *The Library Dragon.* Atlanta: Peachtree Publishers, Ltd.

_____. 1995. *The Last Dance.* Atlanta: Peachtree Publishers, Ltd.

_____. 1997. *The Secret of Old Zeb.* Atlanta: Peachtree Publishers, Ltd.

EHLERT, LOIS. 1989. *Eating the Alphabet: Fruits and Vegetables from A to Z.* San Diego: Harcourt Brace.

_____. 1990. *Color Farm*. New York: Lippincott.

_____. 1990. *Color Zoo*. New York: The Trumput Club.

_____. 1990. *Feathers for Lunch*. San Diego: Harcourt Brace.

_____. 1991. *Red Leaf, Yellow Leaf*. San Diego: Harcourt Brace.

_____. 1993. *Nuts to You!* San Diego: Harcourt Brace.

_____. 1994. *Mole's Hill: A Woodland Tale*. San Diego: Harcourt Brace.

FOX, MEM. 1983. *Possum Magic*. San Diego: Harcourt Brace.

_____. 1985. *Wilfrid Gordon McDonald Partridge*. Brooklyn, NY: Kane/Miller Books.

_____. 1987. *Hattie and the Fox*. New York: Bradbury.

_____. 1989. *Koala Lou*. New York: Harcourt Brace.

_____. 1990. *Shoes from Grandpa*. New York: Orchard Books.

_____. 1993. *Time for Bed*. San Diego: Harcourt Brace.

_____. 1994. *Tough Boris*. New York: Harcourt Brace.

_____. 1995. *Wombat Divine*. San Diego: Harcourt Brace.

GRAY, LIBBA MOORE. 1993. *Dear Willie Rudd*. New York: Simon & Schuster.

_____. 1993. *Miss Tizzy*. New York: Simon & Schuster.

_____. 1994. *The Little Black Truck*. New York: Simon & Schuster.

_____. 1994. *Small Green Snake*. New York: Orchard Books.

_____. 1995. *My Mama Had a Dancing Heart*. New York: Orchard Books.

HENKES, KEVIN. 1993. *Owen*. New York: Greenwillow.

_____. 1996. *Lilly's Purple Plastic Purse*. New York: Greenwillow.

HOPKINS, LEE BENNETT. 1989. *People from Mother Goose: A Question Book*. San Diego: Harcourt Brace.

_____. 1993. *Hand in Hand (An American History through Poetry)*. New York: Simon & Schuster.

_____. 1997. *Marvelous Math: A Book of Poems*. New York: Simon & Schuster.

HOUSTON, GLORIA. 1988. *The Year of the Perfect Christmas Tree: An Appalchian Story*. New York: Dial.

_____. 1992. *But No Candy*. New York: Philomel.

_____. 1992. *My Great Aunt Arizona*. New York: HarperCollins.

_____. 1994. *Littlejim's Gift: An Appalachian Christmas Story*. New York: Philomel.

LAMINACK, LESTER L. 1998. *The Sunsets of Miss Olivia Wiggins*. Atlanta: Peachtree Publishers, Ltd.

———. 1998. *Trevor's Wiggly-Wobbly Tooth*. Atlanta: Peachtree Publishers, Ltd.

LESTER, HELEN. 1992. *Me First*. Boston: Houghton Mifflin Co.

———. 1995. *Listen, Buddy*. Boston: Houghton Mifflin Co.

LIONNI, LEO. 1970. *Fish Is Fish*. New York: Pantheon.

———. 1994. *An Extraordinary Egg*. New York: Alfred A. Knopf.

LYON, GEORGE ELLA. 1992. *Who Came Down That Road?* New York: Orchard Books.

———. 1993. *Dreamplace*. New York: Orchard Books.

MACLACHLAN, PATRICIA. 1994. *All the Places to Love.* New York: HarperCollins.

———. 1995. *What You Know First*. New York: HarperCollins.

MERRIAM, EVE. 1991. *The Wise Woman and Her Secret*. New York: Simon & Schuster.

———. 1993. *12 Ways to Get 11*. New York: Simon & Schuster.

POLACCO, PATRICIA. 1992. *Mrs. Katz and Tush*. New York: Dell Publishing.

———. 1994. *My Rotten Redheaded Older Brother*. New York: Simon & Schuster.

———. 1996. *Aunt Chip and the Great Triple Creek Dam Affair*. New York: Philomel.

RYLANT, CYNTHIA. 1982. *When I Was Young in the Mountains*. New York: E.P. Dutton.

———. 1983. *Miss Maggie*. New York: E.P. Dutton.

———. 1985. *The Relatives Came*. New York: Bradbury Press.

———. 1988. *All I See*. New York: Orchard Books.

———. 1992. *An Angel for Solomon Singer*. New York: Orchard Books.

———. 1996. *The Old Woman Who Named Things*. San Diego: Harcourt Brace.

SCHERTLE, ALICE. 1994. *How Now, Brown Cow?* San Diego: Browndeer Press.

———. 1995. *Down the Road*. San Diego: Browndeer Press.

SCIESZKA, JON. 1989. *The True Story of the Three Little Pigs*. New York: Viking.

———. 1991. *The Frog Prince, Continued*. New York: Viking.

———. 1992. *The Stinky Cheese Man and Other Fairly Stupid Tales*. New York: Viking.

_____. 1995. *Math Curse*. New York: Viking.

VAN ALLSBURG, CHRIS. 1985. *The Polar Express*. Boston: Houghton Mifflin.

_____. 1986. *The Stranger*. Boston: Houghton Mifflin.

_____. 1988. *Two Bad Ants*. Boston: Houghton Mifflin.

VIORST, JUDITH. 1971. *The Tenth Good Thing about Barney*. New York: Atheneum Publishers.

_____. 1972. *Alexander and the Terrible, Horrible, No Good, Very Bad Day*. New York: Atheneum Publishers.

_____. 1978. *Alexander, Who Used to Be Rich Last Sunday*. New York: Atheneum Publishers.

_____. 1981. *If I Were in Charge of the World and Other Worries*. New York: Aladdin Books.

_____. 1995. *Alexander, Who's Not (Do You Hear Me? I Mean It!) Going to Move*. New York: Atheneum Publishers.

_____. 1995. *Sad Underwear*. New York: Atheneum Books for Young Readers.

WOOD, AUDREY. 1984. *The Napping House*. San Diego: Harcourt Brace.

_____. 1993. *Rude Giants*. San Diego: Harcourt Brace.

_____. 1994. *The Tickleoctopus*. San Diego: Harcourt Brace.

WOOD, AUDREY AND DON. 1984. *The Little Mouse, the Red Ripe Strawberry, and the Big Hungry Bear*. Child's Play (International) Ltd.

Interesting Perspectives on *The Three Little Pigs*

CELSI, TERESA. 1992. *The Fourth Little Pig*. Austin: Raintree Steck-Vaughn.

LOWELL, SUSAN. 1992. *The Three Little Javelinas*. Flagstaff, AZ: Northland Publishing Co.

SCIESZKA, JON. 1989. *The True Story of the Three Little Pigs*. New York: Viking Kestrel.

TRIVIZAS, EUGENE. 1993. *The Three Little Wolves and the Big Bad Pig*. New York: Scholastic.

Other Good Stories to Share

ALEXANDER, LLOYD. 1992. *The Fortune-Tellers*. New York: Dutton Children's Books.

AYLESWORTH, JIM. 1992. *Old Black Fly*. New York: Henry Holt and Company, Inc.

BANKS, SARA HARRELL. 1997. *A Net to Catch Time*. New York: Alfred A. Knopf, Inc.

BARASCH, MARC IAN. 1991. *No Plain Pets.* New York: HarperCollins.

BEIL, KAREN MAGNUSON. 1992. *Grandma According to Me.* New York: Doubleday.

BOTTNER, BARBARA. 1992. *Bootsie Barker Bites.* New York: Putnam.

BOULTON, JANE. 1994. *Only Opal.* New York: Philomel.

BOYD, CANDY DAWSON. 1995. *Daddy, Daddy, Be There.* New York: Philomel.

BRADBY, MARIE. 1995. *More than Anything Else.* New York: Orchard Books.

BRUCHAC, JOSEPH. 1993. *The First Strawberries (A Cherokee Story).* New York: Dial.

CARLSON, NANCY. 1996. *Sit Still.* New York: Viking.

CAZET, DENYS. 1990. *Never Spit on Your Shoes.* New York: Orchard Books.

CHRISTELOW, EILEEN. 1994. *The Great Pig Escape.* New York: Clarion Books.

CURTIS, JAMIE LEE. 1993. *When I Was Little (A Four-Year-Old's Memoir of Her Youth).* New York: HarperCollins.

DICKS, IAN AND DAVID HAWCOCK. 1993. *Them Bones: A Fabulous Four-Foot, Fold-Out, Pull-Out Skeleton.* New York: Delacorte Press.

EMBERLEY, ED. 1992. *Go Away, Big Green Monster!* Boston: Little, Brown & Co.

EVERITT, BETSY. 1992. *Mean Soup.* San Diego: Harcourt Brace.

FALWELL, CATHRYN. 1993. *Feast for 10.* New York: Clarion Books.

FAULKNER, KEITH. 1996. *The Wide-Mouthed Frog.* New York: Dial.

GIOVANNI, NIKKI. 1994. *Knoxville, Tennessee.* New York: Scholastic.

GREENFIELD, ELOISE. 1988. *Nathaniel Talking.* New York: Black Butterfly Children's Books.

HOFFMAN, MARY. 1991. *Amazing Grace.* New York: Dial.

HOWARD, ELIZABETH FITZGERALD. 1991. *Aunt Flossie's Hats (and Crab Cakes Later).* New York: Clarion Books.

HUTCHINS, PAT. 1971. *Titch.* New York: Macmillan Publishing Co.

INKPEN, MICK. 1993. *Penguin Small.* San Diego: Harcourt Brace.

JAHN-CLOUGH, LISA. 1994. *Alicia Has a Bad Day.* Boston: Houghton Mifflin Co.

JAMES, SIMON. 1991. *Dear Mr. Blueberry.* New York: M.K. McElderry Books.

JAQUITH, PRISCILLA. 1995. *Bo Rabbit Smart for True: Tall Tales from the Gullah.* New York: Philomel.

JOHNSTON, TONY. 1994. *Amber on the Mountain.* New York: Dial.

KIRK, DAVID. 1994. *Miss Spider's Tea Party*. New York: Scholastic.

KNOWLES, SHEENA. 1988. *Edwina the Emu*. New York: Harper Trophy.

LESTER, JULIUS. 1994. *John Henry*. New York: Dial.

LEWISON, WENDY CHEYETTE. 1992. *Going to Sleep on the Farm*. New York: Dial.

LOCKER, THOMAS. 1997. *Water Dance*. San Diego: Harcourt Brace.

LONDON, JONATHAN. 1992. *Froggy Gets Dressed*. New York: Viking.

MARTIN, BILL, JR. AND JOHN ARCHAMBAULT. 1988. *Listen to the Rain*. New York: Henry Holt.

MCBRATNEY, SAM. 1995. *Guess How Much I Love You*. Cambridge, MA: Candlewick Press.

MCNAUGHTON, COLIN. 1995. *Suddenly*. San Diego: Harcourt Brace.

———. 1997. *Oops!* San Diego: Harcourt Brace.

MCPHAIL, DAVID. 1993. *Santa's Book of Names*. Boston: Joy Street Books.

MELMED, LAURA KRAUSS. 1993. *The First Song Ever Sung*. New York: Lothrop, Lee & Shepard Books.

MOON, NICOLA. 1995. *Lucy's Picture*. New York: Dial.

MUNSCH, ROBERT. 1996. *Stephanie's Ponytail*. Toronto: Annick Press.

NEWTON, LAURA P. 1986. *Me and My Aunts*. Niles, IL: Albert Whitman & Company.

PALATINI, MARGIE. 1995. *Piggie Pie*. New York: Clarion Books.

PHILPOT, LORNA AND GRAHAM. 1994. *Amazing Anthony Ant*. New York: Random House.

PINKNEY, GLORIA JEAN. 1992. *Back Home*. New York: Dial.

RAHAMAN, VASHANTI. 1997. *Read for Me, Mama*. Honesdale, PA: Boyds Mills Press.

RANKIN, LAURA. 1991. *The Handmade Alphabet*. New York: Dial.

RASCHKA, CHRIS. 1993. *Yo! Yes?* New York: Orchard Books.

RIDDELL, CHRIS. 1990. *The Trouble with Elephants*. New York: HarperCollins.

RINGGOLD, FAITH. 1991. *Tar Beach*. New York: Crown Publishers, Inc.

ROSEN, MICHAEL. 1989. *We're Going on a Bear Hunt*. New York: M.K. McElderry Books.

RYDELL, KATY. 1994. *Wind Says Goodnight*. Boston: Houghton Mifflin.

SCHOLES, KATHERINE. 1990. *Peace Begins with You.* San Francisco: Sierra Club Books.

SCHROEDER, ALAN. 1995. *Carolina Shout!* New York: Dial.

SCOTT, ANN HERBERT. 1967. *Sam.* New York: McGraw-Hill.

SPINELLI, EILEEN. 1992. *Thanksgiving at the Tappletons'.* New York: HarperCollins.

STEPTOE, JOHN. 1987. *Mufaro's Beautiful Daughters (An African Tale).* New York: Lothrop, Lee, & Shepard Books.

STEVENS, JANET. (Adaptor and illustrator.) 1995. *Tops and Bottoms.* San Diego: Harcourt Brace.

STICKLAND, PAUL AND HENRIETTA. 1994. *Dinosaur Roar!* New York: Dutton Children's Books.

THOMAS, VALERIE. 1987. *Winnie the Witch.* Illustrated by Paul Korky. Brooklyn, NY: Kane/Miller Book Publishers.

TILLER, RUTH. 1996. *Wishing.* Atlanta: Peachtree Publishers, Ltd.

UNICEF. 1989. *A Children's Chorus: Celebrating the 30th Anniversary of the Universal Declaration of the Rights of the Child.* New York: E.P. Dutton.

VAUGHAN, MARCIA. 1995. *Whistling Dixie.* New York: HarperCollins.

WATSON, MARY. 1995. *The Butterfly Seeds.* New York: Tambourine Books.

WATSON, PETE. 1994. Illustrated by Mary Watson. *The Market Lady and the Mango Tree.* New York: Tambourine Books.

WILLIAMS, SHERLEY ANNE. 1992. *Working Cotton.* San Diego: Harcourt Brace.

YOUNG, ED. (Adaptor and illustrator.) 1993. *Moon Mother: A Native American Creation Tale.* New York: HarperCollins.

_____. 1992. *Seven Blind Mice.* New York: Philomel.

Easy Readers and Early Chapter Books

Bank Street Ready-To-Read Levels 1, 2, and 3

Published By Bantam Little Rooster Books.

Level 1

The Color Wizard
A Dozen Dizzy Dogs
The Gruff Brothers
The Rebus Bears
Things That Go: A Traveling Alphabet
Wake Up, Baby!
Who Goes Out on Halloween

Level 2

Annie's Pet
Follow That Fish
Hedgehog Bakes a Cake
Moon Bay
"Not Now!" Said the Cow
You Are Much Too Small

Level 3

A Horse Called Starfire
Lion and Lamb
Lion and Lamb Step Out
The Magic Box
Mr. Bubble Gum

Dell Yearling Books

For a complete listing of all Yearling titles, write to:

1540 Broadway
New York, NY 10036

By Judy Delton

Bad, Bad Bunnies
Blue Skies, French Fries
Camp Ghost-Away
Cookies and Crutches
Grumpy Pumpkins
Lucky Dog Days
Peanut Butter Pilgrims
Pee Wee Christmas
The Pee Wee Jubilee
Pee Wee Scouts
Pee Wees on Parade
The Pooped Troop
Rosy Noses, Freezing Toes
Sky Babies
Sonny's Secret
Spring Sprouts
That Mushy Stuff
Trash Bash

HarperCollins Children's Books

10 East 53rd Street
New York, NY 10022

By Betsy Byars

Good-bye, Chicken Little
The Pinballs
The Seven Treasure Hunts

Bantam Doubleday Dell Publishing Group, Inc.

1540 Broadway
New York, NY 10036

By Leonard Kessler

Old Turtle's Baseball Stories
Old Turtle's Soccer Team
Old Turtle's Winter Games
The Worst Team Ever

By Barbara Ann Porte

Harry in Trouble
Harry's Mom
Harry's Visit

By Tony Johnston

The Adventures of Mole and Troll
Happy Birthday, Mole and Troll
Mole and Troll Trim the Tree
*Night Noises And Other Mole
    and Troll Stories*

By Andrew Brown

Gus and Buster Work Things Out

By Marjorie Weinman Sharmat

Nate the Great and the Boring Beach Bag
Nate the Great and the Fishy Prize
Nate the Great and the Halloween Hunt
Nate the Great and the Lost List
Nate the Great and the Missing Key
Nate the Great and the Musical Note
Nate the Great and the Phony Clue
Nate the Great and the Snowy Trail
Nate the Great and the Sticky Case
Nate the Great Goes Undercover
Nate the Great Stalks Stupidweed

By Patricia Reilly Giff

The Kids of the Polk Street School (Series)
New Kids at the Polk Street School (Series)

NOTE: there are several books in these
two series.

Other books
by Patricia Reilly Giff

The Beast in Ms. Rooney's Room
The Candy Corn Contest
December Secrets
Fish Face
The Fourth Grade Celebrity
The Gift of the Pirate Queen

The Girl Who Knew It All
Have You Seen Hyacinth Macaw?
Left-Handed Shortstop
Loretta P. Sweeny, Where Are You?
Love, From the Fifth Grade Celebrity
The Mystery of the Blue Ring
The Powder Puff Puzzle
Rat Teeth
The Riddle of the Red Purse
The Secret at the Polk Street School
The Valentine Star
The Winter Worm Business

Works Cited

ALLEN, R.V. (1976). *Language experiences in communication.* Boston: Houghton Mifflin.

FLETCHER, R.J. (1993). *What a writer needs.* Portsmouth, NH: Heinemann.

TRELEASE, J. (1982). *The read-aloud handbook.* New York: Penguin.

PATERSON, K. (1995). *A sense of wonder: On reading and writing books for children.* New York: Plume/Penguin Books.

PETERSON, R. & EEDS, M. (1990). *Grand conversations: Literature groups in action.* New York: Scholastic.

WEAVER, C. (1994). *Reading process and practice: From socio-psycholinguistics to whole language.* 2nd ed. Portsmouth, NH: Heinemann.

Author

Lester Laminack is professor and head, Elementary and Middle Grades Education, at Western Carolina University in Cullowhee, North Carolina. He teaches graduate and undergraduate courses in literacy and is actively involved in state and national literacy organizations. He has published several books in his field, including *Learning with Zachary* and *Spelling in Use.* Lester Laminack has recently published two children's books, *The Sunsets of Miss Olivia Wiggins* and *Trevor's Wiggly Wobbly Tooth.* He is an active member of the National Council of Teachers of English and has contributed essays to NCTE journals *Language Arts* and *Primary Voices.* He is a former member of the Whole Language Umbrella Board of Directors and is also active in the International Reading Association. He has served as a consultant to Literacy Volunteers of America since 1987. He is an author, a teacher, and most of all a learner.

*Composed by Precision Graphics in Adobe's ITC Cheltenham
and Cheltenham Condensed with display lines in Adobe's Nueva.
Printed on 60-lb. Lynx by IPC Communication Services.*